THE DON'T SWEAT GUIDE
FOR NEWLYWEDS

Other books by the editors of Don't Sweat Press

The Don't Sweat Affirmations
The Don't Sweat Guide for Couples
The Don't Sweat Guide for Graduates
The Don't Sweat Guide for Grandparents
The Don't Sweat Guide for Parents
The Don't Sweat Guide for Moms
The Don't Sweat Guide for Weddings
The Don't Sweat Guide to Golf
The Don't Sweat Stories
The Don't Sweat Guide to Travel
The Don't Sweat Guide to Weight Loss
The Don't Sweat Guide to Taxes
The Don't Sweat Guide for Dads
The Don't Sweat Guide to Retirement
The Don't Sweat Guide for Teachers

THE DON'T SWEAT GUIDE
FOR NEWLYWEDS

Finding What Matters
Most in the First Year

By the Editors of Don't Sweat Press
Foreword by Richard Carlson, Ph.D.

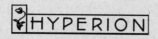

New York

Hyperion books are available for special promotions and premiums.
For details contact Hyperion Special Markets, 77 West 66th Street,
11th floor, New York, New York 10023, or call 212-456-0133.

ISBN: 0-7868-9054-1

FIRST EDITION

10 9 8 7 6 5 4 3 2 1

Contents

Foreword

Near the top of the list of exciting times in one's life is that of becoming a newlywed. For many, it's a time of extreme connection and deep love. The future seems so bright and full of promise. There's no question that a new marriage is a gift—and to recognize it as such makes it even more so.

Interestingly enough, however, being a newlywed almost always lends itself to at least a little added stress in one's life. Make no mistake about it, most people are more than willing to take the trade-offs, as the joy often greatly overshadows any downside. Yet there's no denying the fact that some stress exists in most cases. The simplest reason for the stress is pretty obvious. You're now two people sharing a life. This means you can't do things exactly the same way you've always done them. In the vast majority of cases, there must be some compromise and adjustment. The way you do certain things may be quite different from the way your new spouse does them. You may view chores and/or free time quite differently. You may have different expectations about everything from spending time with old friends to paying the new joint bills to what it means to have a clean house.

How do you approach an issue or bring up a delicate subject? Do you tend to communicate directly? Or do you approach subjects a little more carefully?

In my opinion, the editors of Don't Sweat Press have done a beautiful job in addressing these (and many other) issues. I like how this book addresses sensitive and important issues in a lighthearted way that lends itself to non-defensiveness. If anything, I think this book will help you act like a team!

The Don't Sweat Guide for Newlyweds is a simple yet strong collection of strategies designed to give you and your new partner some powerful tools to work with. I think working with this book will be not only helpful but fun, as well. While you go through it, I hope you'll recognize the importance of the role your own thinking and attitude play in the creation of your marriage. You have the power to make it work.

Kris and I just celebrated our seventeen-year wedding anniversary. As I read the strategies in this book, I was certain that reading them when we were newly married would have been extremely helpful. Marriage is a gift to be treasured and nurtured. I hope you will find, within this book, ideas that will help you nurture this special relationship. I hope that seventeen years from now, you'll be as happy as Kris and I have been able to be. Good luck, and congratulations.

Richard Carlson
Benicia, California, 2003

THE DON'T SWEAT GUIDE
FOR NEWLYWEDS

1.

From This Day Forward

Every marriage is likely to have its ups and downs. As you relish the excitement of preparing for your wedding day and the glory of the wedding itself, you'll surely feel destined for a lifetime of wedded bliss. But it is helpful to remember that marriage is a landscape of hills and valleys.

A marriage often becomes something for which you find yourself unprepared. When two people come together to marry, they join together as partners not just for life but *in* life. The reality is that when two people decide to tie the knot, there are other forces that end up directly influencing their marriage—sources that they might not have initially considered. Family members, friends, and coworkers can all end up playing key roles in your relationship.

Like it or not, from this day forward, you'll be the recipients of volumes of unsolicited advice. You'll need to prepare yourself for how to handle your responses tactfully and keep the peace. Learn to take such advice with a grain of salt, learn to stand up for what you believe in, and always remember the reasons that brought you and your beloved to the altar in the first place.

Bottom line here—the decision to marry should be somewhat similar to deciding to ride the world's largest roller coaster: Make sure that you're prepared for all the ups and downs, twists and turns, but above all, be sure that you're both securely fastened in at all times!

2.

Committing

Why do couples marry? Well, for love, obviously! But many couples who love each other deeply believe that it's still possible to share their lives together without making it "official."

Couples who cohabitate need to realize that living together is not at all like getting married. Young couples who choose cohabitation over marriage often make the mistake of believing that there really isn't a difference. In fact, there are many differences. Living together is considered to be more stressful than getting married. Why? Less commitment!

It's also believed that couples who live together may not discuss important or troublesome issues in their relationship. The end result is that these couples are more likely to break up. This is why it's important to weigh the pros and cons of living together and not marrying before either of you packs a single bag.

Discuss with your beloved your reasons for getting married. One *right* reason for getting married is that you're in love with one another. Also, you both have a desire to share your lives together. People who marry desire a lifelong companion who's not going to bail when things get a little bumpy.

Be sure that you both have realistic expectations—and *similar* expectations: a willingness to fulfill one another's needs and desires and a commitment to support one another, no matter what. Couples who choose to live together share these things, too, but in the end, it all boils down to one thing: With the commitment of marriage, a couple is much more likely to work out differences later on down the road instead of throwing the relationship away and moving on.

3.

For All the Wrong Reasons

Marriage is a big step. It is possible, however, to get carried away in the excitement of it all: "If we get married, we'll get to have a big party and invite all our friends! It will be a blast!"

True, it *will* be a blast. There are few events as thrilling and beautiful as a wedding. But it's essential for both of you to look past the affair. Focus instead on the reasons that you want to marry, and be sure that they are the *right* reasons. There are many wrong reasons to marry.

The party is just a party. Granted, it'll be one heck of a bash, but it will eventually end. Sure, it's always nice to be showered with gifts, but in the end, it's all just "stuff."

Young couples in love are always looking for time that they can spend alone, especially if each is still living at home. But getting married just to have a little couple alone time is a bad idea. Though marrying will give you a new sense of maturity and freedom from your parents, if you're not really ready to commit, don't do it for this reason. It's important to examine whether you're getting married just to "play house," or if you're truly ready for a committed relationship.

Loneliness can be a powerful impetus for wanting to marry. However, marrying for the sole purpose of not wanting to be alone is setting your relationship up for failure.

If you're a couple dealing with an unexpected pregnancy, and you're really not ready for marriage, other alternatives should be discussed. A baby is a huge responsibility that requires the care, love, and nurturing of two people who also love one another. Were you planning to marry anyway? Then move the date up and good luck to you. However, if your relationship is a new relationship, or if you aren't in love, work together to explore other options than marriage. Bringing a new baby into a loveless marriage is asking for problems from the get-go.

Money is the hands-down *worst* reason to marry! Money is a quick fix to your financial troubles, but honestly, if you or your beloved has financial troubles *now*, what makes you think that there won't be big money problems in the future?

4.

To Register, or Not to Register?

The subject of registering for wedding gifts is a touchy one, not only for the bride- and groom-to-be, who may feel uncomfortable with the practice of asking for presents, but for their family and friends, as well. In reality, registering for your wedding or engagement gifts is not only an extremely helpful practice, but it saves time and money in the long run.

There will surely be numerous calls from your parents and friends about what you need to set up house, what your tastes are, or where they can shop for you. Having an answer at the ready will save you time and stress. Registering takes the guesswork out of gift giving.

Remember, however, that it still isn't going to be smooth sailing after you register. It's important to keep in mind a few suggestions when registering.

Stick to department stores or chains that offer online gift registry. This way, everybody can have access to your wish list.

Think practically. You may feel silly registering for a twenty-five-dollar ice bucket or a vacuum cleaner, but you'll eventually need both! Make a list of what you think you'll need before going to register. This is a good time to take some advice from family and friends who are already married. They're the best sources for what goods and appliances are ever actually used by newlyweds.

Keep your expensive tastes within reason! Register for "wish" items, in addition to everyday items that you'll get a lot of use out of. Give your guests the option to buy you things that you want without compromising their own limitations.

5.

Sit Down Before Standing Up!

Before you even send out a single invitation, an essential part of beginning your lives together involves having a heart-to-heart with your fiancé. There are certain subjects that ought to be discussed before becoming newlyweds.

Total honesty is essential at this time. Your goal is to discuss your expectations, your hopes and dreams, and your plans for the future. Bringing up these subjects—even the intimidating ones—before beginning a marriage will save you a lot of grief later on. Ask what your partner thinks a marriage is and what he or she believes your roles are. You may think that you know already, but there are bound to be some surprises in store.

You may find out some things about your partner that you didn't know before: how he or she feels about having and raising children, handling your money, or household roles. Things won't always work out smoothly, but as long as you know what you are working toward, and work together toward that goal, it won't split you apart later on in your married life.

Talk about what expectations you have in marriage. Who do you see as the stay-at-home parent? What will you do with your finances? Who will be responsible for certain household chores? Do you have hopes of buying a home? Knowing beforehand will give you a better chance of working toward a mutual solution later on.

The paradox of marriage today is that so many young couples want long-lasting, happy marriages, yet so many end up with just the opposite. Marriage counselors believe that the reason for this failure is due to a misunderstanding of marriage from the beginning and an avoidance by young couples of taking the time to talk it all out before exchanging vows. Shared goals, struggles and sacrifices, teamwork, and the comfort of working together on mundane tasks are what forge strong marital bonds.

6.

Name-Change Stress

It's hard to imagine—especially for the groom-to-be—the stress that's involved with changing a surname. While it isn't as common as it used to be, the majority of brides still opt to leave their original surnames behind and adopt their husband's.

Men, if your bride-to-be is contemplating taking your surname, prepare yourself for the stress that she will undoubtedly have because of it, and give her all of the support that you can during the process. For a woman who has lived her whole life sharing her name with her loving family, the change can become quite emotional.

Once you have your marriage license, you can begin the tedious process of changing your name on all your important documents. For the bride-to-be, minimize your name-change stress by preparing yourself. You're not abandoning your family by giving up your surname; instead you're creating a new name with your new family.

For women who plan to hyphenate or keep their original surname, your stress levels may be even higher, but don't become discouraged. You'll still have plenty of documents to change and paperwork to complete, but you'll also have the added stress of those who are sitting in judgment of your decision. Keep in mind that this is a decision you'll live with for the rest of your life. It's a private choice, and once you make it, you shouldn't have to explain your reasoning to anyone.

For all brides-to-be that are hyphenating, keep one other important factor in mind: The children that you may have in the future may be recipients of your hyphenated name. So if the combination of surnames is cumbersome, you may want to save them a lot of aggravation and choose one surname or the other for them to share!

7.

Wedding-Morning Stress

When the big day finally arrives, suffice to say that it's going to begin *early*. Hair, makeup, dressing, transportation—by the time that you take your vows, you'll feel as though you've been awake for days!

There's no real way to eliminate all of the stress associated with the morning of your wedding. But you can be prepared and organized. About a month before your wedding date, make up a timetable, working backward from the precise time of your nuptials. Include a checklist of what needs to be done, when it needs to be done, and how much time each task will take.

Most important, inform your wedding party of plans well in advance. Bridesmaids, groomsmen, flower girls, or ring bearers should all have a clear idea of their responsibilities and expectations beforehand.

Contact your photographer, videographer, DJ, or band the night before your wedding. You'll feel more relaxed and confident if you confirm that they haven't forgotten, or that they know how to get to the reception and at what time they need to start.

Schedule a ten-minute breather for yourself in the midst of all the preparation! It can be taken separately or alone, but it should definitely be taken! Use the time to practice deep breathing exercises, meditate, pray, or just sit and do nothing! Prepare yourself for the rest of the day, which you can bet will be a whirlwind of activity.

8.

"I Do, Right?"

Couples on the verge of marriage rarely seize moments between rehearsal dinners and gown fittings to contemplate any inner turmoil that they may be experiencing. It's completely normal for both brides and grooms to experience a variety of conflicting emotions during this time, and these feelings usually manifest themselves in strange, sometimes unpleasant, ways.

Arguments may become a common occurrence. Couples planning their wedding—supposedly the happiest day in their lives—frequently find themselves arguing over things that they never dreamed they'd argue over. Tensions run high, and little spats often turn into full-fledged battles. Perhaps you're questioning your love—and your partner's love for you. Pangs of uncertainty can plague you.

Just remember, all of these feelings are completely normal! The level of anxiety increases dramatically as you make your way toward your all-important walk down the aisle. But more often than not, after the "I do's" are finally said, you will experience a huge sense of relief.

9.

Take a Moment

The vows have been exchanged, and the happy couple has retreated back down the aisle. Let the festivities begin!

This is it—the time to enjoy the day that you've been planning, thinking about, and anticipating all of your lives! But before you get too caught up in all of the merriment, you need to find some time— even for just a few minutes—to relish the experience with your new spouse...alone.

Grab your spouse, and slip off to a quiet spot away from the excitement. In some cultures, there is time set aside exactly for this purpose—for the bride and groom to be alone directly after their nuptials. Make this part of your ritual, as well.

Congratulate each other. Share a laugh, kisses and hugs, or just a few tender moments to let the reality sink in. You did it! Before the feelings of euphoria begin to fade, or before your guests begin to leave, you owe it to yourselves to enjoy the emotional day just between the two of you. The day flies by so quickly that if you don't make a conscious effort to create the time alone, it won't happen.

10.

Surviving the Wedding

"**W**edding Fog." It is a term coined by former brides-in-the-know who've experienced the sensation at their own weddings: the foggy sensation of knowing that your wedding is happening, but still being caught up in the worrying over what will go wrong or what hasn't been done to your satisfaction. While it's seemingly impossible to completely eliminate wedding fog, there are steps that you can take to help you enjoy your wedding day the way that it was meant to be.

Spend some time alone with your new spouse. This is a great way to bring yourselves down to earth during the chaos and excitement of the day.

Stop worrying about your appearance. You look beautiful! Inner happiness is the greatest beauty treatment of all.

Take time to visit with all of your wedding guests. Your guests will appreciate your efforts to see that they are having a nice time.

Enjoy your wedding! Now that the day has finally arrived, go ahead and marvel at your place settings, get out on the dance floor, and take a few bites of your meal!

Let things go. There are always glitches, problems, and oversights at a wedding. Prepare yourself for the unexpected, and then move on. In the grand scheme of things, tablecloths, seating arrangements, and flowers don't matter. Your wedding is still amazing, and you're still marrying the person of your dreams!

11.

So, When Are You
Going to Have Kids?

Admit it: You want to scream at the top of your lungs every time someone asks you that question. Bet you even heard it once or twice on your *wedding day*, right? Now that you're newly wed, chances are that you'll be hearing it even more on a regular basis.

Yes, it's intrusive. And yes, it's annoying. It's also insensitive, nosy, and completely inappropriate! Questions like this can cause problems within and without your marriage.

As inappropriate as it may be, newlywed couples are still faced with this question from good friends, close relatives—sometimes even complete strangers! There's no way to avoid the inevitable— society wants you to have that baby, and have it ASAP! If you're not ready (and most newlywed couples are *not*), you'll need to work together on developing a system for answering in a way that won't hurt or offend but will let others know that it's simply none of their business!

Don't be overwhelmed by the pressure that society puts on you to have kids right away. If you're smart, you and your spouse discussed the prospect of children before you were married, so you know each other's expectations. Stick together and stick to your guns where this is concerned, and plan according to *your* schedule—not anyone else's. Having children changes everything in a relationship—if your relationship has just begun, you'll want to get to the point where you feel secure as a couple before bringing another party to the table.

It's easy to fall into the trap of feeling pressure to have children right away—couples want to have kids while they are still young, or while their parents are still energetic enough to enjoy grandchildren. If you've made a decision with your husband or wife to wait (or not to wait) to have a baby, nothing anyone says or asks should affect that decision.

12.

After the Last Wedding
Guest Leaves

The "happiest day of your lives" is over. The band is packing up, the waitstaff is clearing the tables, and the last of your wedding guests are lining up to wish you well and say goodbye.

Though you're most likely off on your honeymoon, bound for some much-anticipated excitement and romance, you may also want to prepare yourself for a little something known as "wedding postpartum." It can happen the moment that the last guest leaves, the moment that your plane takes off for Hawaii, or even months down the line when you're watching your wedding video for the first time.

In the days, weeks, and perhaps even months following a wedding, many couples experience the blues. The day that you planned for months and prepared yourselves emotionally and financially for is over. With nothing to plan for anymore, and with no big event to look ahead to, you can expect feelings of emptiness and loss.

In fact, there is much to look forward to. You have your whole lives ahead of you! You have the relative calm of getting back into your normal routines, with the added excitement of learning to live together as a couple and enjoying all of the pleasures being part of a happily married, newlywed couple brings.

It's perfectly normal to experience a sense of melancholy and loss after a wedding, or any other big event or affair. Obviously, you knew the champagne parade wouldn't last forever. You may have anticipated that you'd feel some sense of sadness when the day ended, but as you approach your honeymoon—and the weeks following—cut yourselves a little slack! Realize that settling back into normalcy is going to take time and a little patience.

13.

Collect Souvenirs

You may want to collect little items during your wedding that you can keep for later on. Sure, you'll have your wedding photographs, your video, and some pressed flowers for albums, but there are other items that you may want to consider saving, as well. Such items may not seem so sentimental now, but years later, you'll be overwhelmed with emotion to look at them.

Your place card, for example, is something that you'll want to save. You could include an engraved napkin with your names and wedding date, an extra party favor from someone who didn't show up, or a copy of your best man's toast. At home, after the honeymoon, visit your local craft store and buy (or make) a memory box to hold these wedding souvenirs. You can use your memory box as a beautiful addition to your new living room, or seal it up and hide it away for opening on your ten-year anniversary! You will be amazed how tiny scraps of memory can trigger feelings that you had long forgotten about.

14.

Scratch the Limousine

When planning a wedding, many of us tend to be as extravagant as we're able, convinced that this day has to provide the best and most elegant in ambiance and service that there is. Of course your wedding *is* an event that you'll (hopefully) have only once, and you want it to be picture-perfect in every way possible. But it may surprise you to know that when the majority of newlywed couples were asked after their weddings to tell the one thing that they would do differently, the most consistent answer was "spend less."

Though it's hard for many of us to look into the future and predict what our lives will be like when we are married and have children, it isn't difficult to imagine that we're going to need money. Perhaps the best piece of advice that you can follow when planning a wedding is to cut costs wherever and whenever possible. When all is said and done, many weddings can end up costing tens of thousands of dollars—money that can be better put to use on a down payment for a new home, a new car, or a baby's future.

Couples can cut costs in many, many ways when it comes to weddings—all it takes is a little compromise. If the flowers that you absolutely have to have aren't seasonal, is it really reasonable to spend so much money on something that won't last? Take a step back for a second, and ask yourself if the cost of buying summer-only roses for a winter wedding is really a cost that you can afford. All flowers are beautiful when they are arranged elegantly in a table centerpiece. It won't take anything away from the fact that you're going to have a beautiful wedding should you go with less expensive, rose-like peonies instead. Discuss a good substitute with your florist.

Make comparison lists for every item or service that you'll be paying for at your wedding. Include a "wish list" and an "acceptable alternatives" list. Total each list and see how much money you can save with acceptable alternatives and still be happy. Is it a few thousand dollars? Well, now you've got yourself a nest egg.

15.

Remember the Needy

The worst thing to witness at a wedding is the enormous waste that takes place, especially when it comes to food. Of course, you never can know who isn't going to eat their dinner or who might not show up at your wedding. But when it comes to preparing and serving food at a wedding, the wedding couple can avoid wasted money and food by discussing and making arrangements for leftovers with the caterer beforehand.

Consider finding a homeless shelter or soup kitchen that can make good use of the food leftover from your affair. In most cases, the shelter won't be able to come to the catering hall or restaurant to pick up the leftovers, but perhaps you can enlist a friend to volunteer to help. Everything from the cocktail-hour appetizers to the leftover entrees should be assembled and packaged for donation—though this will only happen if you make the arrangements before the wedding.

Another altruistic way to remember those less fortunate during your time of joy is to consider making a donation to charity in honor of your own wedding. Or if you're in a position to do so, ask your guests in lieu of wedding gifts to make donations to the charity of your choice. You may want to try "matching donations," where the bride and groom ask for small donations to a certain charity on the day of their wedding, then agree to match them dollar for dollar.

There are always unconventional ways to remember the less fortunate on the day of your wedding: Instead of flowers for centerpieces, make attractive arrangements out of children's books or school supplies that can be donated to needy schools after the wedding. Or arrange toiletries and flowers together in cellophane baskets for centerpieces, and then donate them to a women's shelter afterward. Remembering the less fortunate on a day of great fortune in your lives will not only help many people in need, but it will make the joyous occasion of your wedding more meaningful.

16.

Don't Break the
Honeymoon Bank

Your honeymoon is an opportunity to spend a considerable amount of time with your new husband or wife away from the realities of everyday life, work, family, and friends. It goes without saying that no matter what destination you choose for your honeymoon, this is an experience that will long be remembered.

So why shouldn't it be the most fabulous vacation that you'll ever take? With a chunk of time off from work and some extra cash stashed away for this purpose only, why shouldn't you go all out? The answer is to go as far as you can without draining all of your savings to make it possible.

The first rule of honeymooning is being in agreement: When planning your honeymoon vacation, you and your partner should be in total agreement about your destination. Compromise on a location that is of interest to both of you. Discuss where you'd like to go and what you'd like to do once you get there. Are you the backpacking type? Are you the laze-around-on-the-beach-all-day type? Look for a location that has it all, such as an all-exclusive club. Such vacation spots are popular with honeymooners because they offer a little something for everyone: sports, dancing, quiet time, sightseeing, and more.

When it comes to cost, just like planning a wedding, list the characteristics of your "dream honeymoon," and then make a list of possible, less expensive alternatives. This trip can easily get blown out of proportion where cost is concerned. The last thing that you want to do is put a strain on your brand-new joint bank account. You *do* deserve a heavenly honeymoon, but when you make your plans, look beyond the short span of your trip. You're going to return home from your honeymoon in a euphoric, loving mood— why spoil it when the honeymoon bills arrive?

17.

Honeymoon Expectations

Your honeymoon is a special time and should be the perfect culmination of all of your wedding festivities. It should be something exciting and romantic that you'll remember for a lifetime. Perfect honeymoons don't just happen; they require careful, advanced planning.

Begin planning about six months in advance. Set a budget, discuss with your partner whether you want to save or splurge, and begin investigating possible destinations. Talk with friends or travel agents about locations that might be perfect for both of you.

Talk to your partner about your honeymoon expectations. Working out your expectations in advance will go a long way toward making your dream honeymoon a reality.

Consider how much time you'll be able to take off from work, since this will be a huge factor in choosing your ultimate destination. Consider the climate of your destination and hotel accommodations in the area. What time of year are you going away? In places where there are big seasonal changes, you can expect big price changes, too.

Once you've decided on a honeymoon destination, book early! Make all of the arrangements now—airfare, hotel, even restaurant reservations. It may seem like a lot of work in the short run, but when you arrive effortlessly at your destination, free from further responsibilities, you will be glad that you planned in advance.

18.

The Closest Time of Your Life

Your honeymoon will be some of the closest, most intimate time that you and your new spouse will ever share. Not every couple knows how to be close, though.

Granted, when couples marry, they have a pretty good idea of what closeness is all about or they wouldn't be part of a couple in the first place. But until a couple removes themselves from their daily lives and experiences to a faraway place where it's just the two of them all the time, they haven't experienced true intimacy. For many couples, the honeymoon is the first time that they'll spend an extended period of time alone together.

Sharing a small room somewhere far from home for a whole week can be daunting for some. You automatically learn things about each other that you never knew. He flosses six times a day? She takes a half hour to dry her hair in the morning? Consider it an introduction to the rest of your lives and embrace it all. It's the perfect time to learn what true closeness is all about.

Sharing a honeymoon is *not* like sharing a marriage—at least in a marriage you can have some regrouping time alone. On your honeymoon, it's just the two of you for many days, every day, every meal, and every activity!

Don't let it scare you, though. Instead, think of this time to explore ways you and your lover can become even closer—through intimacy, talking, or even by simply sharing a sunny balcony and reading. Closeness doesn't necessarily mean that you have to be touching or holding hands constantly—it's also about learning when someone that you care for needs his or her own space.

19.

We're Newlyweds!

Once the plane has taken off and you're headed for a far-off destination, it will hit: You're married! You're a newlywed! The best part is that the fun has only just begun.

People love newlyweds. Complete strangers, upon hearing that there are newlyweds in the vicinity, will flock to wish you well! You'll witness it firsthand right there on the airplane: Tell the flight attendant that you were just married, and watch how quickly the word spreads. Maybe it's because newlyweds have that aura of young love, optimism, and happiness around them—something special that makes others want to share in their joy.

Take advantage of all these good wishes and enjoy the attention. Let people in to share your happiness. Accept their gifts graciously, and remember, as soon as you return home, you'll just be plain old Mr. and Mrs.!

20.

Make New Friends, Too!

Some of the best friendships ever formed in the lives of many couples have begun during their honeymoon vacations. Maybe it's the carefree atmosphere where happiness prevails that creates a ripe opportunity for meeting new couples who share similar interests. Or maybe it's the desire for a newlywed couple to have new "couple" friends to pal around with. But the fact is that friendships formed during this exciting time in your lives—even long-distance relationships—can remain forever.

When we think of honeymooning, most of us immediately think of romance, travel, and constant togetherness! Make a point on your honeymoon to venture out of the hotel room to meet new people, too, taking the pressure off spending every waking minute alone together. You can remain holed up in your room all day with your new love, but the time will eventually come when you're going to want a meal or to participate in an activity that will be more enjoyable to share with new people.

As you and your honey honeymoon, you'll be meeting new friends, and in some cases, creating international friendships. Plan a reunion before saying goodbye to your new friends—perhaps on your first anniversary. It'll be a fun way to recreate the good times that you shared on your honeymoon and a fabulous way to create new memories, too!

21.

When the Honeymoon Is Over

The honeymoon has ended and you're settling into married life together back in the "real world." Suddenly, you're noticing things you never noticed about your mate before—like the amount of new shoes she buys in a month, or the fact that he likes to strike up conversations while you're engrossed in a television show. Little annoyances begin grating on your nerves, and often, your spouse may seem more like an inconsiderate roommate than the love that you married a short time ago.

Many couples report that the first year of marriage is the most difficult. The commitment, which at first seemed so exhilarating, can begin to feel suffocating. You may experience feelings of disillusionment, disappointment, or even anger. You wonder if maybe you've made a mistake. Are you falling out of love?

Relax. It's perfectly natural to harbor these feelings! You're not alone in having doubts—your spouse is most likely having them, too—but as reality crashes with your expectations of each other

51

and of marriage itself, you can both find yourselves experiencing feelings of frustration.

The first year of marriage is often a busy time with many transitions. You'll spend time involved in regular, mundane tasks—cooking, cleaning, shopping, driving. Be aware that this is *not* quality time. The first rule of surviving the newlywed stage is for a couple to continue to date! Make time for each other as you did before, and do the things that you did together before the wedding. The initial years of your marriage are your first years of "forever together." They can contain some bitterness, anger, and disillusionment, but that holds true with all of the friendships in your life. The truth is that maintaining a good relationship is just plain hard work.

Love does not come easily. Your feelings may come and go, and there will be days when you will not like your spouse so much. Before your harbored feelings turn into full-fledged resentment, build upon the firm foundation of the commitment that you made, and prevent these potholes early on to ensure that the closeness and caring you experienced on your honeymoon will stand the test of time.

22.

Wedding Postpartum

Be prepared for the newlywed blues. It's an awful thought—to be sad and blue so soon after marriage—but it's hard for anyone to keep up with the frenzied, all-encompassing, joyous pace of a wedding and honeymoon.

All weddings and honeymoons must come to an end at some point, and life goes on. The healthiest thing that you can do to avoid being hit hard by wedding postpartum is to prepare yourself for its arrival.

It's normal to feel depressed and agitated after the wedding and the honeymoon, and normal to find that marriage may not be exactly what you imagined. In the back of your mind, you may have hoped that the novelty of being newlyweds would never end. But there are ways to stretch out the novelty. Stop thinking about how your marriage should be, or where it's going. Instead, savor where it is *now*.

What no one tells the happily married couple is that it often takes time to learn what a marriage is and what it isn't. How could you, unless you've been married before, know exactly what to expect?

While you may want to dwell on the special feelings and memories of your romance, you'll need to discover a balance between living in your dreams and reality. The transition period is a time of growth and discovery. A couple must work at keeping love alive amidst the daily routines of life. Courtship was a time of fun and enjoying each other's company without total obligation. Now living together and functioning together must be learned. A change this major can throw you off balance—both physically and emotionally.

The good news is that most newlyweds have a wonderful first year of marriage. The even better news is that once they've grown accustomed to their new lives, their new mates, and their new responsibilities, their marriages often get better and easier with time.

23.

Make Thanks a Group Effort

One of the biggest sources of stress for a newlywed couple, believe it or not, involves sending out thank-you notes! The happy couple is appreciative of all that's been bestowed upon them, but with the new adjustments that they're dealing with, their return to work and to their regular chores and responsibilities, there tends to be a limited amount of time left at the end of the day.

Writing out thank-you cards—an act that almost always falls on the bride—can be truly time-consuming, especially when there's a desire to personalize each and every one. Quite honestly, there's no reason that the responsibility for writing out thank-you cards should fall on just one half of the newlywed couple! Gift-givers and guests at the wedding were from both sides of the family, and gifts are no doubt being enjoyed by both the new bride and the new groom. So it makes sense for a newlywed couple to come up with a system of thanking their guests that they can both take part in, and one that fits easily into both their busy lives. The rule of thumb here is for you and your new spouse to divide and conquer.

Begin writing as soon after the wedding as possible. Many times, guests are left wondering if their gift was received, or if it perhaps got lost in the shuffle of envelope exchanges at the wedding. Print out a copy of your guest list, and then write each gift received next to the name of the gift-giver. Then split the list in half, select a quiet night with no other distractions, pour yourselves a glass of wine, and start writing!

24.

Tips for Newlyweds

Wedding traditions can be beautiful, romantic, and fun, but they can set couples up for disappointment afterward. The day-to-day work of a marriage is nothing compared to the work involved in finding the perfect wedding cake or the perfect gown. Couples need to remember that what they are really doing during their engagement is preparing for a lifelong marriage.

Remember your goal as you enjoy your wedding experience: building a sustainable, satisfying marriage. When the wedding is over and you've settled into a routine in your new home with your new spouse, keep in mind that your marriage—your relationship— is going to take work.

Remember that you're in it together. Marriage can be a tough transition, because it involves a significant mind shift for both people. For example, when that moment of realization comes for the first time that you can't just "go home" because you're angry, bored, or frustrated, you'll be more than a little startled. Then there's the realization that you can't make weekend plans now without factoring in another person. Of course, you don't need to do *everything* together, but you do need to be responsible to someone else in a new and different way.

Maintain boundaries where family is concerned. You're going to need to put up a united front. Making decisions together and sticking to them is crucial for the good of the marriage.

Compromise. It's truly the key to all good relationships! Think about which differences you can accept and live with, and which you cannot. Remember that your partner, too, will have to make many compromises in order to live with *you*.

Negotiate. Even if you were a couple for years before marrying, there is a significant amount of renegotiating that should take place after your wedding. Your time together, your time apart, money, sex, housework—it all needs to be divided in an acceptable way that both people feel is fair.

Couples who experience serious problems compromising, negotiating, or maintaining boundaries may need to address more complicated issues like power, gender dynamics, and family history. But for the most part, these new rules to live by should come easily if you both happen to be two fair-minded individuals in love. Just remember to accept each other's differences. Try to balance what irritates you about your partner with what you love about your partner. Like you, your partner has strengths and weaknesses.

Also, keep your expectations in check. Ask yourself if they are indeed realistic. Unrealistic expectations will no doubt lead to disappointment, anger, and resentment.

25.

Couplehood

The wedding day has come and gone. So has the honeymoon. In fact, it's been a few weeks into the marriage thus far, and the happy couple is settling into living together in this new dimension of their relationship. Everything is wonderful. Now, how can they make it last?

Continue to appreciate the special qualities that originally attracted you to your mate. During the courting period, you took time to pay attention to the uniqueness of your significant other. Why should that all end after marriage?

Don't expect your mate to know what you expect! Husbands and wives are not mind readers. People tend to think that others know what they imply or what they are thinking. Then when expectations are not met, disappointment and frustration set in. *Ask* for what it is that you desire. Allow your mate to choose if he or she can fulfill the request. Communicate with words and with listening. Many challenges, arguments, and frustrations can be avoided if couples merely share their thoughts and listen to one another.

Make time for each other. Continue dating your mate, and you'll get to know even more about him or her. Couples don't stop getting to know each other because they're married. Exploring new activities together will help build upon your relationship, too.

Share loving words every single day. Be consistent with small gestures of love, too—it's nice to be remembered throughout the year and not just on special occasions.

Finally, keep your sense of humor. Laugh more, and you'll experience the joys of everyday life together.

26.

A Couple Of . . .

Relationships constantly change. Couples often fear that these transitions are a sign of growing apart, but in fact, they are actually opportunities to get closer.

Take the "we" part of couplehood, for example. Of course you're both still giddy over being the new Mr. and Mrs., but that doesn't mean that you have to spend every waking moment together. Couples often think that they should enjoy all of the same things, have all of the same interests, and enjoy going to all of the same places. That just isn't the case. It's nice to share many interests with your new wife or husband, but you both also need to remember that you are individuals.

The expectation of endless togetherness can put unnecessary strain on your marriage. It helps to be honest, and if you're yearning for a little breathing room, express that.

Of course, during your lives together, there are some obligatory events that require time and energy from both of you. But separating for a while to carve out time for yourselves on a weekly or daily basis can be beneficial for your marriage. Plus, you'll have the added excitement of exchanging your experiences later on that evening.

Couples in their first year of marriage need to ask themselves an important question: Who are we as a couple? In exploring the answer together, you'll define your relationship. You'll examine how you relate to each other, how you relate to the outside world, how you handle conflict, and how you meet your own and your spouse's needs.

27.

A Little Love Exercise

Is love enough? We all need to love and to be loved, yet finding and sustaining an intimate relationship can be one of life's greatest challenges. Love is necessary—but not all that it takes to have a satisfying and lasting love relationship. With such a high divorce rate these days, love often fades in the face of irreconcilable differences and accumulated resentments.

Nearly everyone has fears about his or her capacity to love or find the right partner. Even when you've found the right partner, doubts about him or her being the right one surface on occasion.

To create a great love relationship, you must become a skillful communicator in the complex language of the heart. Love may not be enough, but it's certainly a great place to start! With that added security of being loved and feeling love for your partner, you can begin to build upon your relationship and your marriage to withstand even the toughest challenges. Love is at times accompanied by hurt, anger, and frustration. It comes with the territory. Remember that underneath the anger is hurt, and underneath the hurt is love. Loving and caring make one vulnerable. In addition to love, you'll need respect, caring, nurturing, and understanding from your partner.

Ask yourself if you and your partner freely reveal to each other who you really are and what you really want—strengths and weaknesses, hopes and fears, successes and failures. Next, make a list of qualities that your ideal love partner would have—all of the attributes that you would like him or her to have. Now review your list. Of these qualities, how many do *you* possess?

Specific love exercises like this will help you discover that in exercising your "love" muscles, your love will grow stronger with practice. A great relationship doesn't just happen—you create it.

28.

The House Hunt

Couples aren't waiting for the wedding to house-hunt these days—the trend, according to real estate experts—is for newlyweds to buy *before* they get married.

Obviously, it's no easy task to search for the perfect home and plan a wedding at the same time. But when engaged couples know what they want and can afford, and the interest rates behave in their favor, it can be well worth the added stress.

If you and your partner are looking for your first home, plan carefully, and research everything from neighborhood to school district, especially if you plan to start a family in the not-so-distant future. True, it's not traditional to buy first and marry later, but there are other options if you're opposed to cohabiting before saying your vows. One of you can move into the house before the wedding and begin fixing it up or renovating so that it's ready by the time you're married. Then when the wedding and honeymoon are over, the happy couple has a new, finished place to call home.

It's important that couples discuss their credit histories before taking a step toward buying. If one partner has bad credit, it can mean the difference between approval for a home loan and a letter of rejection. Couples typically sign both names on papers associated with the house, including mortgages and offers to purchase. An exception to this rule is if one partner has bad credit, which means that it makes more sense to put the loan under the other partner's name.

Other than credit histories, another aspect that a lender takes into consideration before determining approval for a loan is how much money a couple has saved or how much money they received as gifts.

Another trend these days is to put down as little as possible—anywhere from five to twenty percent of the cost of the house. This way, a couple just starting out doesn't have to break the bank after an expensive wedding and honeymoon, has a new place to move into, and still has a little extra for safekeeping.

Some say that buying a home and moving are two of the most stressful situations that a person can go through—including marriage and childbirth! Don't rush when it comes time for you to investigate your future living arrangements. Do your homework—and be more than a little picky. Compromise is always nice, but it would be a big mistake to buy a house that you don't want.

29.

The New Place

Anyone who has ever moved in with a significant other knows the chaos that can result from that unavoidable "his" meets "hers" scenario. Twenty-odd years of collecting stuff as individuals means one thing for sure: Problems *will* arise when it comes time to combine your belongings into one humble abode.

Before you move one carton into your new place, discuss with your spouse your vision for each and every room. If your home has an ample amount of rooms, no doubt it'll be easier to accommodate you both: He can have freedom in "his" work/play area, and she can have hers. On the other hand, if your home is a starter home or apartment, you'll have a more difficult task. You don't want to upset the balance of power by suggesting that one person's taste is better than the other's, but you'll have to come to some sort of compromise.

Granted, there will be plenty of arguing between newlyweds in order to provide a peaceful coexistence between your combined collectibles. Your ultimate goal is to create an environment that reflects both your personalities and is warm and inviting for your guests. Rest assured that you'll probably have to part with one or two of your favorite items—but overall, you want to provide a home that both of you feel happy and comfortable living in.

Decorating your love shack can seem like a daunting challenge at first, but don't be intimidated. Just like most everything else in a relationship, successfully decorating as a couple requires a little give and take—and a little creativity—but the results are well worth it. Even the most unlikely pairings can live together happily ever after—just like you and your new mate!

30.
Bye-Bye, Bachelor Pad!

For many newlywed couples, moving into a new home to live together for the first time means each person is moving out of his or her own place. In many cases, this means leaving a place considered to be a haven, free from the responsibilities of sharing or taking anyone else into consideration. They made the rules, and they could follow them—or not.

When couples begin to live together, the first few months can be like an experiment—how much distance do two people need to be together and still be comfortable without stepping on one another's toes? Or how can sharing the responsibilities of chores be a fair setup for both?

When you move in together as a married couple, the question of "personal space" becomes an issue. It can be difficult to figure out how to coexist peacefully. Couples on the verge of living together need to figure out a way that they can still stick to what they're used to without infringing on the other's style of living.

Embracing your new living arrangements is undoubtedly going to be an adjustment. While compromise is still the key, *consideration* is also necessary. When you consider that people don't change overnight—and sometimes they don't change at all—you're going to have to look deep inside your soul to determine what you can and can't live with. There are definitely some bothersome idiosyncrasies that some of us just can't let go of, but the important thing is to discuss what they are with your partner and give him or her the chance to work on making adjustments.

Living together is a trade-off and a compromise—you'll need to work at coming up with a mutual agreement for each to let go of one or two annoying habits. It'll free your lives from the smaller stressful situations that can plague a marriage and help you learn to live together happily in your new home.

31.
Moving Day

Whether you're moving down the road, or moving cross-country, moving in general is one of the most stressful experiences that you'll ever have. It's helpful to anticipate that a move won't run as smoothly as you hope it will. Try arranging a "Countdown to Moving Day" list and checking off each item that you accomplish. Establish a file for all moving papers and receipts.

Two months before you move, obtain a floor plan of your new residence, decide what household items you want to keep, and then begin an inventory of all your household goods. Solicit estimates from several moving companies, and contact your insurance agent to find out if your homeowner's policy covers your possessions during the move. Eight weeks before moving is the perfect time to choose a mover.

Six weeks before you move, begin a search for good health-care professionals in your new location, obtain a school district report (even though you may not have children), and fill out post office change of address cards. Send your new address to anyone that might need it—insurance agents, credit card companies, magazine subscriptions, friends, and relatives.

Take a day to clean out closets and dispose of all the items that you will not be taking with you. Before you throw them away, consider donating them to a local charity, or have a garage sale and earn some extra cash!

A month before you move, purchase or borrow the necessary moving supplies: boxes, twine, labels, and so on. When you've assembled them all, start packing. If your mover is doing the packing, arrange for it to be done one or two days before loading begins. A good suggestion is to send furniture, drapes, and carpets out for repair or cleaning at this time.

Make sure to gather valuables and personal papers that you may need immediately in your new home, including medical and dental records and birth certificates. This box shouldn't go with the movers, but should stay with you or be moved in your car. If you'll need a place to stay during the move, now is the time to make arrangements.

Three weeks before you move, arrange to have utilities (gas, electric, phone, cable, water) disconnected in your present home, and connected at your new home. Prepare your car registration and insurance records for transfer and notify the state motor vehicle bureau of your new address.

The week before you move, transfer all bank accounts, cancel your newspaper delivery, and stockpile enough medication to last at least two weeks. Have prescriptions forwarded to a pharmacy at your new destination.

Two days before you move, finish packing. Defrost and dry refrigerators and freezers to be moved. On moving day, be on hand to answer questions and give directions to movers. Be sure to accompany the driver and take inventory of your household goods upon arrival. Read all documents very carefully before signing, and make sure that you have your copy of the bill of inventory. Before the truck leaves your old home, take one final look through the house to make certain that nothing has been left behind, and then double-check that the driver has directions to your new home!

As your items are being delivered, supervise the unloading. It is a federal law that interstate movers must be paid before your goods can be unloaded.

Finally, check carefully for any damaged or missing items. Make a note on the inventory of any damaged boxes or obvious damage to unboxed items before you sign anything!

32.

Decorating Compromises

How do you avoid the inevitable problems that will arise when two people come to live and decorate one home? Well, you can't avoid them all. Different people have different expectations of how their home should be, and learning to accept those differences is the best that a couple can do to avoid difficult situations.

If you have the financial resources, consider hiring a decorator to make choices for you. A third party's involvement will take some of the pressure off and give you both new perspectives. Should this option not be feasible, consider doing away with your personal opinions and settling for a third option: Start thinking "ours," not "yours and mine." Design your new home together.

When you first move in together, you'll have to solve a lot of style issues. It'll take some getting used to—having your stuff and your partner's stuff "clash." Once you get used to the word "ours," the rest will fall into place.

Thumbing through furniture or home catalogs and magazines can be beneficial to new couples starting with an empty slate.

Create a folder of tear sheets of all the decorated rooms that you both like. Have a folder for every single room in your new home.

Little did you know that you might end up bickering over fabric swatches, but don't give up hope that you can amicably deal with these snags. Even if you both have very different tastes, working together on creating the home of your dreams will bring out the best and most tasteful sides of you both!

33.

Making It Work

You thought living together would lead to a harmonious, romantic, and ideal home life. You never thought that you'd be a couple that ends up fighting over the remote or bickering over the best way to do the laundry. After a week of cohabitation, your mate may begin to look less like your dream spouse and more like your roommate from hell!

You never truly know a person until you live with them. But before you decide to kick out your new roommate, look for compromising solutions to all your little spats.

If your mate is a slob, delegate the chores. Assign the dedicated duty of your choice, based upon what you think he or she needs to work on. Don't clean up if he or she forgets—it's the only way for a slob to learn a lesson!

If your mate turns every disagreement into an argument, learn to argue fairly. The best thing to do is find time to have a heart-to-heart, without placing blame on anyone or putting the other on the defensive. Don't say things like, "You never" or "You always." Instead, talk about how *you* feel when a problem arises. Next, after you express your concerns, give your spouse time to answer. Don't interrupt or defend yourself—give your partner a chance to express his or her own feelings. Most important, every time you have a spat, remember to appreciate each other's good qualities.

Payment of bills can be a tough situation to organize when it comes to newlyweds, since you'll both be bringing bank accounts to the table—not to mention your new joint account. One way to go is to keep your own accounts and contribute to the joint account based on who works and earns what. For example, you each contribute half of your monthly salary into your joint account, and then pay bills from that account. Another alternative is to pay a percentage of one salary—should there be a large discrepancy between salaries—into the joint account. And though it's a tough task to undertake, try paying the monthly bills *together* each month. This way, you'll both have an idea of what you have in the bank and how much you're spending each month. When one person is designated to be the bill-payer, it can leave the other person completely in the dark as to what the couple's financial situation is.

The best part about living with someone is that you can learn a tremendous amount about yourself. You learn what you like, what you hate, what you can or can't live with, and most of all, how you can resolve conflicts with someone that you care deeply about.

34.

Secrets to a Successful Marriage

However joyous, happy, and wonderful you are before your wedding ceremony, there's something about getting married that can leave both the bride and the groom with unsettled feelings. You or your spouse may feel that upon your return from the honeymoon, things aren't running the way that you thought they would. With high divorce statistics always looming, you can't leave the success of your marriage to fate. You need to find a balance that works for you both.

Marriage is different from living together. Not necessarily better—just different. Both of you will have different expectations of what a "spouse" should be—often basing those expectations on what you saw of your parents' married life. But times change. Our lives are different from the lives our parents lived, and you should expect that your marriage will differ greatly from theirs.

Couples who have success in their marriages are the couples who talked before the wedding about their expectations of one another. If there had been serious disagreement—for example, if she wanted children and he didn't—they might have thought twice about marrying. After the wedding, successful couples need to continue keeping the lines of communication open regularly to keep their new expectations in check. Then if those expectations clash, they can work it out until they reach an understanding and agreement.

A secret to the success of marriage is for couples to keep one another up on a pedestal. It's tempting, once married, to forget to praise your spouse or to be courteous. We tend to stop seeing each other as important and instead start putting other things like work, hobbies, and friends first. Successful couples always keep each other a priority. They are interested in their partners' opinions, they respect their partners' decisions, and they take their partners seriously. When they talk to other people, they speak lovingly about their spouses, and they never take each other for granted.

Learn to resolve conflicts, keep the romance alive, grow with each other, and never stop working at your marriage. Time and a false sense of security can erode even the strongest love. So regroup every once in a while, to make sure that you're both happy with the way things are going. Then you can count on your marriage being one of the successful ones!

35.

Getting Him or Her to Help

Most marriages today are held together by both partners contributing equally to the housework. Both husband and wife should learn to recognize the signs around them that there's work to be done.

Should one-half of the newlywed couple not be sharing one-half of the household chores, it might just be a case of poor communication. Perhaps it isn't that he or she is unwilling to help out around the house, but more that your partner doesn't know what's expected. In order to avoid any misunderstandings, discuss household responsibilities with your partner from the get-go.

Teach him or her specifically, and in detail, what needs to be done and what you expect of him or her. If your spouse tells you that he or she can't recognize what needs to be done around the house, then training is required—as for any new worker—in noticing these things. Be gentle, patient, and helpful by sitting down and making lists of what to do. Above all—and this may be *hard*—tell your spouse how well he or she has done when finished with the task.

Housework doesn't have to be a sore point in a relationship—there are ways to get help from even the laziest of spouses! But letting it go—especially where shared responsibility is concerned—can build resentment in a marriage.

36.

Yikes! I'm *Nagging!*

Nobody starts out being a nag. It's something that just seems to happen over time—when you want things done a certain way and your partner refuses to comply. Before you know it, you're harping on issues without a second thought.

Nagging is horrible. For starters, nagging will only make you feel bad about yourself. It won't even necessarily make your spouse comply. Usually, you end up faced with a partner who rebels against you or ignores you completely.

Before you turn into a nag, take a look at the roots of the specific problem. What's happening to make you think that your spouse is not showing you any respect? Obviously, you expect your spouse to pull his or her weight around the house. But your spouse may genuinely think it's unimportant. He or she may think that a good spouse is someone who is loving, sensitive, successful, and fun to be with. He or she may not realize the importance of keeping a house in order—or especially, how important it is to *you*.

Discuss all of your expectations with your spouse, not only with regard to housework, but also of their behavior—alone and around other people—and your expectations where work is concerned. Explain to your spouse how his or her behavior makes you feel, how you feel disrespected and ignored, and how you despise having to ask for the same things repeatedly. Explain that when you constantly have to remind your spouse of your expectations, you feel like a nag. Talk, then talk some more, and don't stop talking until you're in agreement.

Once you've discussed and agreed on certain issues, you'll both be clear where it is you stand. You may not have managed to work out all of your problems, but the result is going to be a lot more loving than nagging!

37.

Surprise . . . You're Married!

Marriage is full of surprises. You may know your other half intimately, but you are still in uncharted territory when it comes to living as a married couple. There are many surprises in store for you—some that may surface immediately, and others that won't rear their sometimes ugly heads until years down the road.

What surprises you most about being married? Naturally, the answer is different for every married couple. But one of the most common surprises of marriage reported by newlyweds is the amount that they find they each must sacrifice in order to make the marriage work.

Of course, both husband and wife make many sacrifices trying to keep their marriage strong. And there may be times that one feels he or she is sacrificing more than the other. For many, just being asked to make such a huge sacrifice comes as a big surprise.

For some reason, another big surprise for newlyweds is that marriage is fun—especially after hearing about divorce rates, listening to all of the harrowing tales from other married couples, or seeing all of the "save your marriage" books that line the shelves at the bookstore. Most couples simply relish their couplehood and enjoy each other's company. They laugh together, tease each other, and hug and kiss as often as possible. Sure, there are serious sides of life to deal with, too, but for the most part, marriage is fun.

Another surprising thing about marriage that couples face is that married people don't necessarily feel euphorically in love every minute of every day. Not to say that just-married feelings don't last a long time, but newly married couples are often surprised when that feeling fades a little.

More surprises: Your spouse will change over time. So will your relationship. As you grow together as a couple, as you start a family, as you just plain live your life, everything changes just because it *does*.

Luckily, one happy surprise that couples realize after they marry is that in many cases, marriage just gets better and better! Whether you've been married for forty days or forty years and you still find your spouse exciting and fun to be with, consider yourself lucky to have found such a wonderful person!

38.

Marriage Myths

Many myths that surround marriage give couples unrealistic expectations. Disappointment is sure to come for people who are looking for the fairy-tale, happily-ever-after, storybook marriage year after year.

It's surprising how many young, married couples seem disillusioned with their newly wedded state. Perhaps they expected things to be different based upon what they'd heard marriage was all about from others, from what they saw and heard on television—or from society itself.

What do women want in a marriage? According to one survey, the top three things women want in a marriage are someone thoughtful, a husband who is also a friend, and monogamy.

What do men want in a marriage? According to relationship experts, men want someone who loves them, a wife who is also a friend, and monogamy.

What people really seem to value in their marriage is the companionship that comes from intimate knowledge of someone. If you watch television, enjoy classic movies, listen to love songs, or read romantic novels, you may have an image of marriage that is completely unrealistic. Take a look at some common misleading myths about marriage.

Myth: Marriage makes us complete human beings. Reality: A couple complements one another—not completes one another.

Myth: Marriage will end loneliness. Reality: Many married people are still lonely.

Myth: Romance will always be alive and well. Reality: Nearly every relationship experiences highs and lows in the romance department. The challenges of everyday married life can often cloud the romance.

Myth: Marriage makes people happy. Reality: You can't expect your spouse to be your one source of happiness. Personal happiness must come from within.

A good marriage needs love, support, tolerance, communication, realistic expectations, caring, compromise, and a sense of humor to be successful. A good marriage can also survive conflict, disappointment, and most problems. There's no myth about that—it's the reality.

39.

Falsehoods of Marriage

The reality of marriage is a far cry from the dizzy romance that characterizes the engagement and the wedding. It takes a while for young couples to reconcile these two images of married life. One is not necessarily better than the other, as emotions and priorities change as we get older.

The important thing, at the beginning, is not to have any preconceived notions of what marriage is all about. Recognize the difference between the myths and the realities of marriage. The following statements about married life are all false.

- Married couples should do everything together.
- Spouses need to be able to read each other's minds.
- Loneliness will end with marriage.
- Marriage means romance forever.
- Marriage makes a person complete.
- A couple in love has no problems.

- Having money will solve all problems.
- Marriage makes people happy.
- Having a baby will hold a marriage together.
- Arguing destroys a marriage.
- He or she will change once you are married.

Now that you're married, you probably have your own list of marriage myths. Add them to this list, print the list out on your computer, and keep it in a place where you can review it and renew your faith in *your* marriage from time to time!

40.

Respecting Each Other's Privacy

The issue of privacy in a marriage is a very sensitive and real topic that married couples face every day. From day one, couples who are living together for the first time must establish certain boundaries in order to give their spouses the privacy that they rightly deserve. Without this sense of privacy, a spouse may find it necessary to employ secrecy or deception in order to get the privacy that he or she needs.

Everyone needs privacy—there are many parts of a person's life that he or she will never want to share. Delegating the rules for these private moments should be a number-one priority when moving in together.

The same goes for privacy regarding personal belongings. Old diaries, pictures, or letters that have been stowed away should not be investigated. If your spouse has been considerate enough to put these items away, you should respect this part of his or her past. If you have trouble dealing with the fact that these mementos still exist, you may have other problems to work out that are bigger than the issue of privacy.

Disrespecting your mate's privacy or stooping to snooping will eventually lead to disrespect and distrust in your relationship. Better to begin your marriage from a grounded and secure place that encompasses trust and personal space.

41.

The Importance of Compliments

When your husband or wife pays you a genuine compliment, you are getting a wonderful gift. You get reassurance that you're loved and appreciated, and you're made to feel better about yourself. Taking one minute every day to compliment your partner on anything is a quick and meaningful way to express that you care.

Compliments are a way of expressing to your partner that you're noticing the good things—and not just the bad. We tend to only speak up when something is wrong in our relationships.

Compliments should be true and sincere—not to mention timely! Be spontaneous and genuine and avoid complimenting your spouse to make up for an argument or mistake.

If complimenting doesn't come easily to you, think about what makes you most happy about your spouse and start by putting that into words. It can be something that you've always admired about him or her, or something that he or she did that day that was particularly special. Consider your spouse's accomplishments, or things that he or she does every day that you appreciate.

Remember to give compliments without the expectation that you'll receive them in return. Enjoy the experience of giving a compliment and making an obvious impact on the way that your spouse feels about him- or herself. If you *never* receive a compliment from your spouse, it's time for a heart-to-heart talk. You don't have to shower each other with compliments on a daily basis, but the "one compliment a day" theory is a nice one to try—for both of you.

It's also important to remember that many people actually have a hard time *receiving* compliments. Perhaps they feel undeserving or embarrassed, or perhaps the attention makes them uncomfortable. Whatever the reason, should your compliments make your spouse uncomfortable, that's all the more reason to keep at it. Practice saying nice things to each other at home alone. Try not to disagree with a compliment, either. Instead, try the appropriate "Thanks" as a response. It's really all you need.

42.

Overwhelming Support

Lending support to each other is a way to strengthen your relationship, as well as enhance each of your individual successes. It's also a way to help make a stressful time for your spouse that much easier.

As an individual, your spouse may be completely independent—able to excel at a great job, take care of the kids (if children are involved), *and* keep the home in tip-top shape. But the truth is that no matter how much anyone feels that they can do it all, everyone needs a little support now and then.

One important aspect of lending support to your partner is recognizing when he or she needs it but may be too involved or too proud to ask. Whether your help consists of picking up extra chores around the house, giving your spouse some "down time," or talking through a particularly vexing work issue, giving support before your spouse reaches the breaking point will be very much appreciated.

The next time that you find yourself with an opportunity to lend some support to your spouse, grab it! It might be as simple as holding her hand while she makes a stressful phone call, or letting him skip your weekly Sunday yard work so that he can just play couch potato and watch sports. Consider being supportive and do it just that once.

However you choose to do so, giving your time and energy to help make your partner's life a little easier is a generous and loving offer. Sharing in each other's personal endeavors is a way to invest in your future together.

43.

Get to Know Each
Other Even Better!

You dated for years, were recently married, and have been living together for quite some time. You probably know everything that there is to know about one another, right?

Chances are that you don't know everything—or even *half* of everything—about your new spouse! Yes, you know all about your partner's family, and probably much about his or her history. You know all of the big things—the monumental events that went on in his or her life—too. But let's say that you start asking some more specific questions. It's very likely that you're going to hear some fascinating stories and learn some surprising new things.

Pick a quiet afternoon when you both have nothing more to do than laze around the house and get to know each other better. Think about things that you'd never otherwise think to ask. What was your earliest memory? Who was your favorite teacher growing up? Who did you play with in your old neighborhood? These are great memory-joggers and will unleash things that your spouse hasn't thought about in years.

What was the worst trouble that you ever got into? Who were your best friends? How did you spend New Year's Eve as a child? Ask about saddest memories, funniest memories, and most embarrassing moments. Ask for descriptions of old bedrooms, schools, or cars that their parents drove.

It's possible not to know *everything* there is about one another. Have fun with this exercise in getting to know each other better— take turns asking questions and really listening to your spouse's answers. You never know what you'll find out. If you don't ask, you may never know!

44.

Scheduling Time Together

R emember the days back when you were first dating? You and your lover would make special plans to be together.

One common misconception about marriage is that it gives couples more time together. We expect that when we live together and share a life commitment, we'll also share a life! The truth is that it takes a lot of work to find "quality time" amidst the demands of a career, family, and household.

Luckily, it's never too late to schedule some together time for you and your honey. One thing that you can do is take turns planning mystery dates! Mystery dates are the perfect way to keep up the element of surprise in a marriage and spend quality time with your betrothed.

Set aside one night a month for your mystery date, and then one of you should make all of the plans in secret. All you need to tell your spouse is what to wear and what to bring. You can plan for dinner and drinks at an exclusive restaurant, buy tickets to see a classic romantic film, go to a rock concert, or just have a quiet night at home reconnecting!

The best part about mystery dating is that you and your spouse take turns planning. You can each be as creative as you like and dream up activities that your partner would never suspect or would never think of doing.

Weekend mystery dates are especially fun. Plan an overnight in town or whisk your partner away—sometimes, airlines offer super-special weekend deals to Europe. The main component of a great mystery date is that you get to spend some quality time with your partner and you have all of the activities planned out for you. It's easy to fall into a weekend rut when you're a couple, constantly spending your Friday nights bringing in dinner and watching television.

Try to achieve variety by not repeating the same date twice. The bottom line—mystery, spontaneity, and sometimes a little extravagance—can go an awfully long way!

45.

Scheduling Time Apart

Have you ever been out for dinner with your husband or wife and found that you were just out of things to say? Do you sometimes get to the point that whatever your spouse says or does, you find it irritating, but then you feel guilty for being so critical? If you answered yes to those questions, it may be the perfect time for the two of you to share something special in your marriage: some time apart!

As difficult as it is to find time to spend together in a relationship, it can be equally difficult to find time to be apart. During the engagement and the first few years of marriage, there are an inordinate number of appearances to make as a couple: holidays, family reunions, or get-togethers with friends.

Many relationship experts believe—and recommend—that couples take vacations together and separately. A mini-vacation from your spouse gives you a healthy chance to come back refreshed and genuinely excited to see your partner. At first, the notion of spending a week or even a weekend away from your spouse may seem strange. What will others think? Will it ruin our relationship? Am I really entitled to such independence?

In fact, you are entitled to a large degree of independence in your relationship, and truth be told, spending time apart can be the perfect way to strengthen your marriage. By taking the time to nurture yourself, you're actually giving your relationship a chance to grow and thrive. You and your spouse will have so much more to share when you bring individual experiences to the relationship. You'll both learn firsthand why "absence makes the heart grow fonder." Having a little breathing room can turn those irritating habits back into the endearing qualities you once thought them to be!

46.

A Voice-Mail Relationship

In tough financial times, everyone is overworked. Our jobs expect more from us—more hours, more effort, more work. We expect more from ourselves, and the working newlywed couple caught in the chaos can find it hard to find time to be together.

How can you create quality time with your partner when you're both so busy and overtired? Like everything else in your marriage, you'll have to work at this, too.

Look to put each other first. Work should be important but not as important as your relationship. Be selective about the events that you're invited to, especially if they mean taking time away from your time alone with your spouse.

Stay in contact with each other throughout the day. Surprise your partner with a romantic e-mail at work, just to tell them how much you love them. Check in with each other on a weekly basis. Schedule a set time and place, and then make sure to be there, no matter what! Use these scheduled moments to catch up with each other and find out how the week has gone. A weekly check-in can help you connect with your partner again. The same goes with a phone call once during the workday. Nearly everyone has cell phones these days, and a simple "Hi, I was thinking about you" message left on voice mail can be a real boost.

Make it a point to physically connect every day. A kiss or hug, a massage or a quick neck rub are all things that will bridge the distance of the busy day.

Send your husband or wife something nice at work every once in a while: flowers, a card, a latte—something so that your partner will stop and think about how much he or she loves you.

The most important suggestion for making together time during hectic times is, quite simply, just to make the time! Dedicate time—even if you have to schedule it into your planner—in which you'll have one another's full attention. It can be cuddle time, meal time, working out time, or time playing cards or games. Schedule it, and stick to it. Then in spite of your most hectic work weeks, you'll still have those few moments to look forward to.

47.

Keep Communication Lines Open

Anyone who has been married for any length of time surely has stories to tell about how communication can break down in a marriage. Even the happiest couples have fallen victim to this insidious problem. The fact is that you must learn how to communicate effectively if you expect to have a satisfactory marriage.

It's impossible to overemphasize the importance of communication in any relationship. Recognizing why communication breakdown happens at all can be a first step in overcoming difficulties. At the core, communication requires three things: a sender, a receiver, and a message. It sounds pretty simple, actually, but in fact, it's complicated.

Say you are the sender. You have something (a message) to tell your spouse (the receiver). You say it and expect that he or she hears it. Finished, right? There are, however, many factors that can prevent the above-mentioned communication from taking place smoothly.

There may be an inability to hear the message clearly. You may think that your spouse hears what you say, but in fact, he or she may not hear exactly what you say.

There may be a failure to understand the message. Many people have a habit of calling back, "Okay!" to a request, even if they aren't completely sure what has been asked. For optimal communication between you and your spouse, never "call out" a request to your spouse. Try to speak to him or her in close proximity—and always be sure to simplify the nature of your request.

You may both have different perceptions concerning the meaning of the message. This one's a biggie! Pay close attention: When you say something to someone, what they hear is really just what they *thought* you meant. They are going to act upon it based on their perception of what you said. Sometimes, it's the same thing—but many times, it's not. It helps to be clear and precise about what you request of your spouse in any situation.

Distractions, disinterest, poor timing, cultural differences, threats, and ultimatums are all possible factors in the breakdown of communication. So how do you become a better communicator with your spouse? Real communication takes place when you value the person to whom you are speaking and when you articulate your message in clear, respectful tones. By avoiding anger, by accepting the fact that your message may not be perceived *exactly* how you hope it will, and by keeping an honest and open dialogue, you have a good chance at communicating well.

48.

What Did You Say?

Might it surprise you to learn that one of the main reasons couples divorce is because they lost the ability or never had the skills to communicate with one another? It's true, according to divorce statistics, that poor listening skills lead to the breakdown in communication in a marriage. The following are some tips on how to be a more effective, more avid listener.

Never interrupt! Even if you are just aching to throw your two cents into a heated discussion, always let your spouse finish what he or she is saying.

Avoid being judgmental. Keep an open mind, and avoid jumping to conclusions or looking for the right or wrong of what is being said. This is preventing you from listening—from *hearing*—what your spouse has to say.

Avoid emotional reactions. This is hard to accomplish all of the time, especially if you are an emotional person to begin with, but it helps to think before saying anything in response to what your partner is telling you.

Listening should be a priority. Listen to your spouse without planning how you are going to respond. Let go of your own agenda, and focus more on the fact that you need to listen. Turn off the TV, put down the newspaper, or finish the chore that you were doing, and give your spouse your full attention.

Keep it to yourself—unless you are asked! Don't give advice unless you've been asked for it. You can't listen and talk at the same time.

Most important, remember that men and women generally communicate differently. Men often share because they want to give information or solve a problem. Women tend to talk to connect with someone to get information. Women usually talk more about relationships than men, while men are more often concerned about details than women.

Be aware of the nonverbal signs that both you and your partner send out. They can tell a lot about whether you are listening or paying attention to what's being said. These include shoulder-shrugging, change in tone, constantly crossing and uncrossing arms or legs, nodding, not making eye contact, and certain facial expressions and mannerisms. Above all, respect your partner, and respect his or her point of view, even if you disagree with it.

49.

Actions Speak Louder

Here's an interesting fact: According to the experts, only ten percent of the way in which we communicate with people is through the use of words. The rest of our message is conveyed by gestures, expressions, and posture—all of the little signals collectively known as "body language." Like any language, the better we come to understand it, the more effectively we can communicate.

The way that people stand, the gestures that they make, the placement of their hands during a conversation, the expressions on their faces—even the way that they speak—are all clues to how people feel in particular situations. If you learn to decipher these clues, you will have more insight into what your spouse is trying to say, or what he or she is trying to conceal.

Of course, listening intently to your partner is your first priority when trying to communicate effectively. The trick is being able to listen to their words and decipher their body language at the same time.

Understanding and recognizing your own body language is the first step. Before you begin to decipher your mate's body language, teach yourself to adapt your own body language to communicate better. The sound, tone, and rhythm of your speech provide signals about yourself. With a little practice and skill, you can start to give your mate the kind of body language that you want to receive. For instance, using unclear gestures tends to reflect vague and undeveloped thoughts. If you want to come across as forceful, make your gestures similarly pointed and purposeful.

Play a little "I Spy" the next time that you are involved in deep discussion with your partner. Watch his or her gestures carefully, as they can be an index of emotions. If your partner's hand touches his or her body while speaking, it can be signaling a physical or emotional closeness to the topic you are talking about. If the hand moves away from the body, it can indicate distance.

Listen to what your spouse's body is telling you the next time that you have a conversation. It isn't hard to decipher your partner's gestures, and you'll begin each conversation with better communication from the very start!

50.

Warts and All

It's a good guess that if you've been trying unsuccessfully to change things about your partner since the wedding, right about now, you're pretty frustrated. Guess what? People don't change just because you married them.

Choosing to accept someone else for exactly who they are can liberate you from preconceptions. When you make a conscious choice to truly accept your new husband or wife, to understand that those little behaviors that drive you crazy are simply part of the person that you fell in love with, you can finally free yourself of your efforts to change them. Giving up this task will relieve you of the tension that has probably built up between you and your partner because of the pressure that you've put upon him or her to change.

Start by taking a few moments to think about the things that you've been trying to change about your partner. Choose one thing that irks you the most. Then try to acknowledge that your spouse is different from you, and as a result, will naturally do things differently. Consider that there is no right or wrong way to do something; there are merely different approaches. Make a conscious decision to accept your spouse's behavior.

Accepting your loved ones for who they are will ease the tension in your relationship. Instead of approaching certain situations with frustration and anger, you'll approach them with love and tolerance.

51.

Your New Social Life

It's inevitable: Not long after you're married, your social life is going to change. It isn't going to change for the worse; it's just going to *change*.

You'll still have the same friends that you've been hanging with for years, and you're not suddenly going to drop all of your single friends now that you're married. But the bottom line is that a young, newlywed couple needs more than just their old friends. What a young, newlywed couple needs is another young, newlywed couple to hang out with!

Let's face it; as much as you'd like to cling to your past and still consider yourself a swinging single, you have new concerns now. You've entered a world where sharing your hard-earned money with someone else is a major issue. You can certainly go out with the guys or girls, but if they aren't in a position to relate to your situation, finding common ground will be more difficult.

Not that you shouldn't hang with your friends once in a while. In fact, it's essential that you include these friends in your life whenever possible. But if you're making a "things to do after we're married" list, then put high up on the top, "Find another married couple to hang out with."

Another couple will share similar concerns and be going through similar circumstances as you. They know what it's like to be newly married. They know what it's like to suddenly have to share all of the household chores. Best of all, forming a friendship with another couple where you have so many things in common will most likely be a friendship that will stand the test of time. Your children may grow up together, you'll celebrate similar milestones together, and most certainly, you'll vacation together.

There's no way that your single friends or your friends from work are about to travel with you and your two little babies to Disney World for a week. Your couple friends, however? They'll jump at the chance!

52.

Surviving Football Season

A couple can often benefit from sharing common interests instead of letting these interests tear them apart. Getting into whatever your spouse enjoys—watching football, gardening, working out—can mean quite a lot to him or her. With a little research, you can gain just enough knowledge to become involved in your loved one's hobby of choice.

Ask questions when there's something you don't understand or want to learn. Your spouse will find your interest endearing and exciting. You may even end up enjoying your new skill more than your spouse—and now you've established an activity that both of you can enjoy together. The more you can be together, communicate about shared interests, or just have fun as a result of your hobby, the more you'll feel included and connected.

53.

Common Ground

The art of negotiation, most newlywed couples learn, is an essential part of keeping the peace. Everything has to be negotiated—whose turn it is to cook dinner, which sofa to buy, how much money to put into savings—so much so that you may find yourself longing for the days when it was just you making the decisions.

Even if couples have lived together before marriage, there is significant renegotiation that needs to happen almost immediately. The most common areas of negotiation are time together and time apart, money, and housework. Newlywed couples know that the stakes are higher now—and patterns can be quick to form.

When negotiating, look for common ground. Figure out aspects of the issue that you agree upon. Then tease out the areas of difference that need negotiating. Most important, remember to attack the problem and not the person. The latter behavior is childlike and ineffective.

Teamwork is what's important here, and you're on the same team. All too often negotiations become a win-lose situation, and this is destructive. You need to create a nonjudgmental environment in which both partners can keep the goal in mind and remain focused. The only acceptable outcome is one that both husband and wife can live with because it feels fair.

If you get stuck, it may be that there is a deeper issue at work than whose job it is to do something. It may be that you also need to address more complicated issues first in order to get the negotiations back on track.

54.

The Three-Month Anniversary

The twelve-week mark of your marriage is a great time to bust out the photograph proofs and have everyone over for a photo party. Why? Because during the amount of time that has passed, you may have started feeling those pangs of nostalgia over missing your wedding—that event in your life which took twelve months to plan and orchestrate—and you may need to relive the affair!

On your three-month anniversary, treat yourselves to an emotional journey back in time—to gaze longingly at the gown that will never be worn again, marvel over the floral arrangements long since expired, and gush over the happy faces of your wedding guests.

Many wedding photographers are slow to assemble wedding albums—even if they've managed to send you proofs quickly after your wedding. While it may take up to six months for a finished album to reach the eager hands of the happy couple, chances are that you've assembled quite an array of photographs from your wedding from other sources: guests who brought cameras and took pictures, or those instant point-and-shoot cameras that many brides and grooms like to include on each table at their wedding so guests can snap away whatever and whenever they'd like.

One must-have item for newlyweds is a big, fancy photo album for all your assorted photographs that were not taken by the official photographer. Start creating your own wedding album by arranging these photos in chronological order, then assembling them in attractive ways on the pages. Be creative, and think of fun and interesting ways to put pages together. See if certain photos arranged together tell a story or highlight special moments. You may even want to pay a visit to your local craft store for ideas and supplies for making wedding album pages.

Invite friends and family over for an evening of coffee and cake, or wine and cheese. Ask them to bring any other photos from your wedding that they may have—photos perhaps that you haven't seen yet. Pass them around, laugh, cry, or whatever! Exchanging stories and special moments from your big day with the people that you love most will undoubtedly provide you and your spouse with more precious memories.

55.

The First Fight

There's really no such thing as a "first fight" between newlyweds, because chances are that if you've been a loving, committed couple for a while already, you've already had more than your fair share of arguments. It's only natural and healthy for a couple to disagree, but somehow, after you've wed, that "first" argument can seem like a tornado has walloped your relationship. Experts say that money is the leading cause of arguments among newlyweds, with in-laws a close second.

In truth, there is no simple solution to approaching an argument, but reconciling that first argument in a healthy way can be a model for the future. Learning to solve problems effectively early on can only serve you well later.

As you know, compromise is essential in any relationship. Unfortunately, it can also be one of the hardest parts! But when you're faced with the choice between an aggravated power struggle and creating a compromise, choosing compromise will take your relationship in the best direction: toward fairness, intimacy, and above all, trust.

When you and your partner find yourselves faced with a situation in which neither of you seem willing to budge, consider what would really make you feel better—fighting or compromising. But remember, a fight has a way of escalating. It's up to the two of you to either promote those angry feelings and create distance between yourselves, or compromise and bring yourselves back together.

No, compromise isn't satisfying. In compromise, we have to give something up to get something—and that can be hard. But presenting compromise in a fair way to your partner—and avoiding placing blame—will make your road easier.

Remember that compromise is give-and-take. Let go of a little, and so will your spouse. Agree on a fair solution for both of you.

56.

The Second Fight

Every relationship—even the relationships that seem perfect—inevitably brings its share of disagreements and annoyances. As any couple works toward resolving their differences, they will undoubtedly run into an impasse.

Perhaps your partner misunderstands your needs. Perhaps your needs are just not feasible. This can lead to a breakdown in communication and start a tiny spat that can eventually escalate into a full-blown fight. Harsh words get thrown around. Feelings get hurt. Compromise, while often the best way to settle disputes, may not always work when a couple has reached an impasse. When compromise fails, what choice is left?

We all make choices in our relationships. We can choose to take a situation personally and get angry and hurt by it, or we can choose to deal with the problem in a rational manner. There's another method of reconciliation, and it's known as "letting it go." Letting it go may sound like you're giving up—and in some ways you may be—but when your relationship is on the line, it's better to look at the problem realistically and decide whether or not it's *really* worth getting worked up over. If it isn't, then you ought to just work on letting it go.

Letting it go doesn't mean that the matter can't—and shouldn't—eventually be discussed. Your partner owes it to you to hear you out and understand that his or her actions were hurtful. Harboring these feelings will only cause resentment. But choosing to deal with the situation productively—minus the tears, the yelling, and the complaining—will go a long way in the short run.

At a later point, when things are calmer, you can address your partner. Can you come up with a way to explain your feelings—without getting too emotional? Did you, perhaps, have unrealistic expectations of your partner in this case?

Letting go doesn't mean that you can't stand up for what you want or need. It simply allows you to release the painful negative emotions that accompany conflict. Then when you're settled, you can communicate with your partner more clearly and effectively.

57.

Effective Results

Every marriage brings two individuals to the table—two individuals who will eventually annoy each other in one way or another. But what do you do when your differences still feel substantial? What if you discover an impasse that can't be worked through, or a recurring, hurtful situation that just can't be resolved?

When it comes to marriage, we have to learn to accept that we'll all experience threatening situations. They are impossible to avoid. But you can learn to "agree to disagree" and let time bring solutions that may not be apparent at the moment.

You can only have the same argument so many times. Rehashing the issue week after week can make it seem as though your relationship is stuck in some kind of torturous cycle.

When a couple agrees to disagree, and this could relate to issues outside the marriage, too, they can eventually stop having the same arguments and just accept that their partner is different. You may experience a certain sense of loss that you and your spouse are not in sync over everything. But eventually, there will be a peace of some sort, preferable to the tears and harsh words that ensue when you argue about the same thing over and over again.

Disagreements can also be kept in control by practicing role reversal. By taking each other's position regarding an issue or argument, each partner can gain the perspective of their spouse and engage in an enlightening conversation. A couple can learn to appreciate each other's point of view without feelings of anger or defensiveness. When this is achieved, a couple can move on to problem solving, negotiation, and yes, compromise.

When all else fails, ask yourself this question: Why is it so critical that we be in agreement over this particular issue? There's a good chance it's *not*. Agree to disagree. Then accept your partner for his or her opinions, and respect that independence.

58.

Money Management and Marriage

Among the obvious changes that a newlywed couple experiences, that of financial management may be the most crucial. Nearly everything—when it comes to money—becomes a joint decision. It is essential for newlywed couples to plan and coordinate their finances, especially if both husband and wife are wage earners and already have other financial accounts established.

Among the first tasks a couple should undertake is looking closely at their complete financial picture. Set aside time to review both of your incomes and how they are being used. Discuss future goals and their financial implications. All of these dreams take some financial planning, and that planning needs to begin now.

Achieving these dreams may require some drastic changes to how you've become accustomed to spending money! You'll both want to practice discipline in your spending habits from now on, in order to achieve your goals. Step number one is establishing a budget.

For those who've never created or spent within a budget before, be realistic. Find ways to meet your expenses, and set aside a cushion for unexpected ones. Keep close watch, month to month, on your budget to determine what cuts or allowances you may need to address.

Creating a budget for spending is great, but if your budget plan does not include savings and investments for the future, it isn't an effective plan. Think long-term even if you haven't yet begun *talking* about family planning.

Most important, review your needs for checking and savings accounts. Joint checking and savings, separate accounts—whatever you decide, investigate the financial institutions that you put your money into in order to get the best value for your earnings.

Financial management in a marriage requires some monumental decisions, as well. The couple should decide who is going to take care of handling the personal finances. It will be confusing at first— delegating and relinquishing responsibilities where money is concerned may make you feel as though you're also relinquishing control. Work together to divide the tasks at hand, and then sit down together at regular intervals to bring one another up to date. Health, life, and auto insurance policies need review, too, since marital status will most likely change your original policies.

This world of new responsibilities and newly shared financial obligations can be overwhelming. Nevertheless, it's essential that the two of you develop a sound financial plan that includes adequate protection against life's unforeseen risks.

59.

He Spends, She Spends

Financial stress is cited as the number-one cause of divorce in America today. Couples whose fiscal behavior doesn't match up run the risk of falling into stressful times.

When it comes to your money, arriving at strategies that work for both of you is key to surviving the inevitable arguments that you'll have over money. Set up rules from the get-go—rules that work for you both. Talk about your approaches to sharing, spending, and saving money. Discuss the options that suit you best as a couple: sharing bank accounts, or perhaps keeping separate ones. Having it both ways may be best for you so that you'll be able to enjoy some degree of spending freedom.

It helps to set up boundaries where spending is concerned. Say you and your husband agree to discuss any purchase over one hundred dollars, but purchases below that spending limit can be made without consultation. Or you may be the type of couple who works better with assigning each other weekly allowances.

Whatever financial agreements you and your spouse come to, it's important that they be reached unanimously. Marriage is a partnership, and neither husband nor wife should be made to feel inadequate if they must depend on the other for money. It's healthier for a couple to meet somewhere in the middle, giving each a role in their joint fiscal responsibilities.

Sharing a life together also means sharing control. Control over the family funds is power over many aspects of life together, so it needs to be approached in a sensitive way.

60.

Thinking About the Unthinkable

Though it's not a topic that most newlyweds embrace discussing as they begin their lives together, the possibility of dying prematurely and leaving behind a loved one is a topic that no young married person should ignore. The "life insurance" talk should happen as early on in your marriage as possible, as well as certain legal preparations, should the unthinkable occur.

It's hard for young couples to think about life insurance and premature death. In fact, many couldn't tell a life insurance policy from a medical policy. The best way to determine your individual insurance needs is to carefully review your financial situation with an insurance advisor, who can also answer any questions that you may have and offer advice on the policy that best suits you both.

Then ask yourselves some important questions, such as: If you were to leave this earth prematurely, how much would it cost your surviving spouse to meet monthly living expenses or maintain his or her standard of living? Consider all living expenses, mortgage or rent payments, clothing and food, and debt such as credit card bills, student loans, and car loans when figuring on just one salary as income.

It's important to ask yourselves these questions now, because there are certain advantages to purchasing life insurance early in life. If you buy when you're young and healthy, you can lock in coverage and insurability options at favorable rates. For most newlyweds, term insurance is the best way to get adequate coverage at an affordable cost. You can expect to pay more for permanent life insurance, which offers an investment component in addition to death benefits.

Statistically, young married couples are more likely to be disabled than to die prematurely. That's why disability insurance is also important. It provides you with a monthly income in the event that an accident, illness, or injury leaves you unable to work.

Make out a will. Now's the time to decide who you would want to inherit your estate. If you die without a will, your beneficiaries would be those that your state's legislature chose for you. If you have children, a will can help you protect them, as well. If you already have a will, make sure that you quickly prepare and execute a new one after you're married, as your old will, in most states, is no longer fully enforceable.

Compared to planning your wedding or house-hunting for your first home, buying insurance is less than romantic. But coverage that protects you and your spouse against life's unforeseen risks is an important part of planning your life together.

61.

In-Laws

We've all heard it said: "When you marry, you're marrying your spouse, not your spouse's family." The truth be told, when you marry somebody, you are also committing to another relationship: a relationship with that person's family.

Unfortunately, in-laws make poor bedfellows, especially in a marriage. This is mainly because they are not your parents, and likewise, you are not their child. This does not mean that you will never be able to establish a loving, warm relationship with your in-laws—you most certainly can. But during the course of your relationship, be sure to remind yourself from time to time of those facts.

You grew up with your parents, and you've become accustomed to the way that they behave as parents. You can't expect your new "parents" to behave the same way. That said, what you must do as the new daughter- or son-in-law is learn to live with these new people in your life!

For the lucky few blessed with hands-off, accepting in-laws, this will be a cinch. It will be pleasant at holiday time, shared meals will be a joy, and you will be able to create a loving atmosphere with your new family members. But since *most* people experience tension and frustration adapting to a new set of parents, it's in your best interest to learn how to establish a livable, perhaps even enjoyable, relationship with your in-laws.

Remember that they are your spouse's parents. He or she loves them unconditionally—and has for decades. The worst thing that you can do is pit your spouse and in-laws against each other. Your spouse may then have to make a difficult choice as to whom he sides with. Don't put him or her in that position.

Show your in-laws respect from the very beginning. Hopefully, they, too, will understand that respect is a two-way street and show a little to you, as well.

Open your heart and your home to them—to a comfortable degree. It's probably not wise to have your in-laws stay in your home for long periods of time when you first marry. Four adults living in one home can become a source of plenty of tension and aggravation, especially if you are newly married and still learning to live with one other person.

Chances are that you'll enjoy a wonderful relationship with your in-laws for many years to come. Of course, you'll hope that they'll eventually make terrific grandparents to your children and have a relationship with them that is beneficial to everyone. Alienating them early on will cause tension between you all—tension that you don't want to pass down a generation.

62.

Keeping the Peace

The in-law relationship is often a complicated one that will require some practical and philosophical tips for peaceful coexistence. First, accentuate the positive. Surely not everything that your in-laws do is wrong, improper, or inappropriate! Pinpoint those moments, and keep them in the forefront of your mind the next time you're wishing that your in-laws would pack up and move to another state.

Change your expectations. Your in-laws may never turn into the in-laws that you'd hoped for. Just as people have different parenting styles, there are different in-law styles. You can't change them, but you *can* change your perceptions and expectations of them.

Help them keep off your back! In-laws can often be controlling—to the point of total frustration for a newlywed couple. Keep the peace by helping them find a happy medium in their lives—one that will allow them to control smaller, less important things while also offering other outlets for their time.

Don't always feel the need to hold back. Sit down with your mother- or father-in-law and point-blank explain to them what they're doing that's bothering you. Let them know how you're feeling—in the gentlest of words, of course—especially if you've been feeling hurt or angry.

Present a united front. Before you blow up from frustration or cause a rift in your relationship that may never heal, speak to your spouse about your in-laws' destructive or unpleasant behavior. Work out ways to make the situation better, and then present them—together—to your spouse's parents.

You don't know what all the fuss is about? Then good for you! Congratulations—you're part of that fortunate percentage of newly married people who don't have a problem with their in-laws.

63.

A Successful Interfaith Relationship

Research conducted by various religious organizations recently concluded that the primary stress for interfaith couples is the celebration of holidays. Holidays are a challenge to many new couples—regardless of their religious backgrounds. This is even more so the case with interfaith families.

Keep yourselves informed about both religious holidays and family traditions that each of you practiced as children. When a new family member knows little about the practice or tradition of his or her spouse's culture or religion, the insecurity and discomfort that they feel intensifies.

Celebrate together. Obviously, this demands a great deal of preparation and negotiation on both sides. Family members need to be accepting of one another, regardless of their differences. Speak to your parents and relatives before joining a family celebration, and have your spouse do the same.

There is no clear-cut approach to celebrating together that will work for all families, but following one simple rule can help:

Talking about things works, and *not* talking about things does not work! Discuss with your spouse, your family, and your spouse's family what your intentions are and what you expect from them. Respect their decisions to join in and celebrate with you, or step aside from time to time. The end result—whether you can develop a warm, loving relationship between all family members—ultimately depends on you and your family.

Remember that the goal of holiday celebrations is to bring families together, not to create distance. Work together when preparing for the holidays, and try to be sensitive to each other's spiritual needs by looking at the holidays from your spouse's perspective. Above all, when you are deciding which holidays to celebrate and with whom, consider which holidays hold most meaning for you and your partner.

64.

Making Decisions

When you lived alone and you had tough decisions to make, the best part about it was that you didn't need to consult anybody else for their opinion. Now that you are sharing your life with someone else, you'll need to learn how to make decisions as a couple.

If you're two people with similar likes and dislikes, decision-making may be a non-issue. However, if you are one of the many couples who often agree to disagree, decision-making is going to present a challenge!

Not to fear, however. You have love, respect, and communication on your side. You value each other's opinions (however diverse they may be), and you've grown to respect the choices that your loved one has made in his or her lifetime. This shouldn't change now that you are married.

When you and your partner become "stuck" trying to decide something, talk it out. Looking at the issue in a number of different ways may shed enough light to discover the best possible solution.

It may end up being yours, it may end up being your spouse's, or it may end up being neither.

Explore other possibilities, rather than have one of you decide. It will take some getting used to—this new way of living your life. In time you will develop something more important than any one decision: a relationship with someone that you love based on mutual respect and consideration!

65.

Dividing the Holidays

One issue that comes up quite quickly in a new marriage—and one that neither of you can ignore—is the issue of the holidays. Yes, they are meant to be happy times, but you may want to brace yourselves as you approach your first holiday as newlyweds. There are much bigger issues involved now—issues that can literally tear a relationship apart!

Very often, a newlywed couple argues over what to do for the holidays and with whom. Guilt sets in, and with that guilt comes a lot of potential anger.

Don't let it start out this way. Couples often fall into a routine of doing what their parents still expect of them. This routine can carry over for years to come. Take control in your first year, and you'll have control of your own holiday plans from that time forward. Expect that feelings might get hurt and that not everyone is going to be happy with your holiday decisions, but such is life. We can't all be everywhere at once.

Don't cheat yourselves from having a special first "big holiday" together. You'll need to learn the art of splitting up the holidays, now that you're married. If both of your families are having dinner at the same time—and neither will budge on their plans—alternate from year to year. If distance is not a factor, dine with one family and have dessert with the other. Making the rounds at holiday time can be fun, too—popping in here and there to wish everyone well. After all, the actual eating part is not what the holidays are all about. They are about being together.

Young couples should have fun on their first holiday together. The important thing is for you to convey to your families how much you love them, and how much you'll be thinking of them should you decide to spend your holidays alone, just the two of you.

66.

Single Envy

From the very start of our adult lives, we equate being single with independence. It's like nothing that we've ever known before, and we come to experience a deep sense of self.

When we marry, so much of this changes. We begin to separate from the life that we've carved out for ourselves and from the people that we've come to know as "family." It's a confusing time for young adults. Once that ring is on that finger, people begin treating you differently. You're invited different places, assuming that you're now only attending couple functions, or you're *not* invited places where couples are not the norm.

It's confusing because while you may love your new life, you're also experiencing loss—the loss of your old life, the friends that you don't see as much anymore, and the loss of what you knew to be your independence. You may miss the autonomy of making decisions, the opportunity for spontaneity, and the bonding that you shared with your single friends.

This isn't a bad thing, of course. It's just a natural progression. But while you're enjoying your new social life and getting used to your new codependence, it's also natural for you to feel envious of your single friends and long for the way it used to be.

It's important to keep in mind during these melancholy times that single life wasn't always a bed of roses. Surely you experienced feelings of loneliness or pressure to find someone. When single envy hits you every now and then, fight back with the positive things about couplehood. Host a dinner party for all of your couple friends. Or join your single friends on their big night out—then come home to your honey and relish the notion that you have somebody wonderful to love.

67.

Protecting Your Marriage

You made vows on your wedding day. Most likely, you promised to love your husband or wife, even under the worst circumstances. Traditional vows include words like "in sickness and health" and "for richer or poorer," but have you ever noticed that words like "passion," "attraction," and "happiness" are not mentioned? That's because marriage is not only based on feelings, it's based on commitment. Love doesn't come easily, and marriage takes a lot of work.

You may be dismayed to learn that your feelings will come and go, and there will be days when you don't particularly care much for your spouse. You may experience feelings of anger, disgust, disappointment, or exhaustion. Yet based upon the promises that you made a short time ago, you are still expected to love your husband or wife in spite of your feelings. Protecting your marriage will guarantee a love that stands the test of time.

When you are proactive in protecting your marriage, you become aware, almost constantly, of what you say and do in front of your spouse. Behaviors that you and your spouse consciously commit to at the start of your relationship will protect you from heartache down the road. Avoid comments that may make your spouse jealous. Don't bad-mouth your spouse to family or friends or use hurtful words in an argument.

Let go of mistakes. Everyone makes them. Instead, learn from the mistakes that you make as a couple, and allow them to be steps toward your growth.

Protect the passion in your marriage. Keep it alive! Protect the happiness in your marriage. Participate in fun activities together, continue the courtship of your relationship, and go above and beyond to bring joy to your spouse. Tell jokes, share funny stories, and encourage an environment of love and laughter in your home.

Naturally, protecting your marriage is something that you'll both need to work at. One happy person does not a good marriage make. Set goals together—passion and happiness goals, too!—for your relationship. The love and passion that you experience and extend toward one another can last when it's built on a solid foundation. Above all, ensure that your spouse knows that he or she holds a place dear in your heart that no one else can touch.

68.

Marriage and Exhaustion

Most newlywed couples are DINKs when they get married. Being a DINK, or "Double Income, No Kids," has its benefits. One is more money coming in that can be spent a bit more frivolously, as there are no family-related expenses to contend with, such as diapers, schoolbooks, doctor visits, or soccer league fees.

Still, there *are* certain pressures that two-income couples must deal with when both partners are holding down full-time jobs. Exhaustion is one of them.

Newlywed, working couples struggle with the physical and emotional exhaustion of keeping their marriage together and keeping a stressful full-time job. It's an exhaustion that can lead to a total communication breakdown if it's not dealt with in a constructive manner. A new deal needs to be worked out once you marry—a deal that includes sharing the housework and the pressures associated with working full-time equally.

Support is the key here. Understanding that your spouse works just as hard at his or her job as you do, and that he or she may come home in a variety of moods each day, is at the core of making it work. Before you pick a fight over whose turn it is to make dinner or fold clean clothes after a busy day, you may want to include scheduling in some relaxation time for both of you at the end of each day.

Of course, relaxation may mean different things to different people. Respecting one another's means of relaxing is essential when working toward your common goal of keeping it together each night.

Talk about each other's needs and desires. Devise a fair workload schedule that you both can live with—one that will keep the house running and keep you a happy couple, as well.

69.

Out with the Boys

It may take some time to adjust to the dynamics of socializing as a couple. But you don't always want to be in a social situation with another couple. In fact, you may not always want to be in a social situation with your spouse!

Once you're married, you're essentially on a string of dates with your partner 365 nights a year. You're going to reach a point in your marriage—usually early on—when you're going to want to go out and have fun with an odd number of people for a change!

Guys' Night Out (and Girls' Night Out) is an essential part of any relationship. More often than not, a man may need to break away from the couple for a night and bond with other male friends. The healthiest relationships are the ones where Guys' Night Out and Girls' Night Out are part of the routine. These nights apart can, in fact, bring a couple closer together, as they offer an opportunity to miss each other and have new things to talk about afterward. Keep in mind that like any component of your relationship, trust and respect play a key factor in the success of such nights out.

70.

Out with the Girls

Just as it is important for men to experience a little independence every now and then, women deserve the same. There's nothing more rejuvenating to a relationship than spending some "girls only" time apart from your spouse!

Let's face it: There are many topics that husbands usually just don't enjoy discussing. Girls' Night Out provides an opportunity for women to bond with girlfriends and not worry about bringing up topics of conversation that are met with eye-rolling.

As with Guys' Night Out, try making Girls' Night Out a routine event in your life—perhaps taken on the same night as your spouse enjoys a night out. As time goes by, you will find yourself looking forward to this special time alone with your friends. Again, trust and respect are necessary to ensure the success of nights out, and when you and your spouse return home, grateful to have someone waiting for you, you'll remember how valuable alone time is.

71.

Becoming Your Parents

Soon into your marriage, you may suddenly be reminded of another married couple that you know: your parents. Before you can stop it from happening, you may start acting and sounding just like your parents. You may begin to wonder: Am I becoming my parents?

No matter how wonderful our parents were, we often hope that we won't turn out to be like them. We enter into an adult relationship with another with our own designs for marriage—new ways that we want to approach it and fresh, nontraditional ideas for making it unique.

But most surprisingly, many of us end up following in the exact patterns of marriage that our parents set! That's the nature of marriage. Traditional marriages where the husband works and the wife keeps house—as absurd as they initially seem to newlywed couples—often end up being the marriages that they are in. We find ourselves adhering to the traditional practices that we once balked at: dinner at six-thirty every night, weekend shopping for the house, Saturday nights out.

Should you sense that your relationship is beginning to mirror that of your parents', don't fight it. Chances are that you're just duplicating the best parts of your parents' marriage. Certainly, there were some good aspects of your parents' relationship. Strive to repeat those, while working to avoid some of the same problems that your parents faced. By following their patterns, you'll end up knowing what to expect and be able to see any difficulties way ahead of time.

72.

Dreams for the Future

When we were kids, we spent much of our time dreaming about the future. Now, as adults, we're all too aware of what our daily responsibilities are. Don't be afraid to plan for your future or discuss and dream with your spouse about what lies ahead. Many newlywed couples feel strange discussing topics such as getting pregnant or purchasing a home right after they're married for fear that they might be thought of as unhappy in their current situation and desire an immediate change. Or perhaps they don't discuss these things because they just seem so far away.

The future, however, is an important part of your relationship. It should be discussed—and discussed often—since you're hopefully both going on the assumption that it's going to be *forever*. Not talking about the future will only lead to uncertainty in your relationship.

When you do begin discussing the future and where your marriage is headed, think about creating a timeline so that you'll both be on the same page as to what your expectations are.

Discussing the details now will leave you better prepared for making those plans, too.

When was the last time that you and your partner talked about your hopes and dreams? Sharing your deepest desires for the future and dreaming together can bring you closer. Saying certain things aloud can be incredibly powerful, and if you work together, there's no reason that your life can't turn into a dream come true!

73.

Time Apart

Some couples never spend a night apart. Others, due to different circumstances, find themselves away from each other often, or at regular intervals.

For whatever reasons that you and your spouse find for having to spend time apart, be sure to prepare yourselves for all of the mixed emotions that you'll experience! Happiness over the little taste of freedom and independence you'll have, sadness over being alone, fear that he or she might lose interest in you, anger that you couldn't go, too—you may experience them all at once, or one right after the other. Either way, it's enough to make even the tightest relationships a little insecure.

Many people who are part of a new marriage feel apprehensive about spending time apart from their spouses so soon after the wedding. They worry about the feelings of loneliness that they'll experience or the fears they'll have that their relationship will drift apart.

In fact, many couples are surprised to learn how time spent apart from one another actually strengthens their relationship. Sharing individual experiences afterward, giving each other time to miss the other, and counting down to a partner's return can be very exciting in a relationship. Of course, what's best about spending time apart is reuniting and reconnecting—in every way!

Perhaps our apprehension stems from our distorted image of what soul mates are and how much time they need to spend together to be happy. The amount of time that a couple spends together is not a way to measure their marital happiness. Different couples vary in the time that they need to spend together to be happy.

74.

Control—Remote and Birth

Of all the important discussions that you and your partner will engage in after the wedding, there are two that are of the utmost importance: 1) Who will be in charge of the remote control, and 2) Who will be in charge of the birth control? As far as the issue of "control" in your relationship is concerned, the discussions should end there.

When it comes to relationships and marriage, control is considered a four-letter word. Nobody wants to feel as if they're being controlled in a marriage. And nobody wants to ever feel powerless in a relationship. So we often find ourselves stuck.

Yes, there are some things that you may *want* your spouse to control in your life: balancing the checkbook or taking care of the plumbing, for example. But in all other situations, couples should work together on making sure each possesses an even amount of control.

75.

Spend One Whole Day in Bed

There's nothing more relaxing, more exciting, or more extravagant in life than spending one entire day in bed with your spouse. For this reason, and for the sake of your marriage, you owe it to yourselves to spend at least one whole day each year in bed!

Plan it if you must. Or try it spontaneously one morning and play hooky from work. Take a break from all the rushing around, running errands, work responsibilities, and rush hour traffic. Use the time instead to cuddle with your honey, read to each other, relax, listen to music, and have breakfast, lunch, and dinner in bed!

The nice thing about a day in bed is that it slows life down. The only job for the day is to concentrate on enjoying each other's company. It's great to think that while the world is operating in full force right outside your window, the two of you are just lazing around, spending an intimate day together, oblivious to it all. Post your rules for this day from the start: No telephones or e-mail answering allowed, no working, and absolutely no discussion of the myriad household chores that need to be done.

76.

China, Here We Come!

Surely you're anxious to show off that fine set of china that you spent hours pondering over—that's now sitting restlessly in your new china cabinet. Being newlyweds gives you a chance to entertain as you've never entertained before.

If you've never thrown a dinner party, rest assured that it's simple. The best part is that you'll get to spend a lot of time in the kitchen with your new spouse, and work side by side to create something wonderful.

The best dinner party menus are the least time-consuming. Select an entrée that's prepared in advance, and then you can pop it in the oven to warm it up.

Be careful not to overestimate your cooking abilities! If you've never been much of a chef, stay away from recipes that involve wrapping, stuffing, double boiling, or decorating. Instead, look for exciting ways to soup up some old staples, such as pasta dishes or chicken.

Delegate. With two cooks in the kitchen, you're bound to step on some toes during all the preparation. Assign tasks early on so that each partner knows what she or he is responsible for. Then select a work space for each of you to avoid the inevitable crowding.

When your guests arrive, have appetizers ready and waiting. Find one guest eager to be the evening's bartender. Stock your bar in advance, and check to be sure that all of the staples are there.

Most important, make sure that you and your spouse have ample mingling time. There's nothing more unappetizing than having a host couple spend their entire party in the kitchen!

77.

Six Months Later

Many couples get so overwhelmed with attention during their engagement and wedding that when it's all over, they begin to miss it. How can they continue to feel special? By making sure that their marriage is full of fun and festivity every single day.

It's the simple things in life that end up making us feel special. Keep that feeling alive and kicking in your marriage, and you'll be celebrating your romance well after the wedding.

Break out the new china and crystal as often as possible—for friends and family, but also for yourselves. Take a second look at the gifts that you received during your engagement and wedding, and use them to remind you of how you felt when you opened them.

Celebrate the milestones of your marriage as you would celebrate a holiday: After your first big furniture purchase, pop open the champagne. For your first Fourth of July together as a married couple, decorate in red, white, and blue.

Watch your wedding video or crack open your wedding album and look at the photographs in a new light. Examine each of them, searching for things in each picture that you may not have noticed before.

Return to the place that you spent your wedding night—even if it was at a dumpy airport hotel. Or pay a visit to the place where you were married and peek in on another wedding taking place.

There are many ways to keep the magic of newlywed life alive. Turn to each other and look deep within to find the glory and the novelty of your romance. It's up to you and your spouse to make each other feel special—not just for the next few months, but for the rest of your lives.

78.

Get a Dog First

You may feel ready to have a baby, with everything seemingly in place. You have the room for a nursery, you have the savings in the bank, and you have relatives on hand offering extra help. So what are you waiting for? There's much more that a young couple needs to think about before having a child, to ensure that a new baby comes into this world under the best possible conditions.

Get a dog first. Or a cat. Or even a parakeet. Being responsible for another living thing is a huge undertaking, and though many newlywed couples experiencing wedded bliss feel that they are ready for an addition to their family, in fact, they are not. A new baby changes everything—your life, your career, your home, your routine, your couple dynamics—everything. While a new pet is *not* a substitute for a new baby, at least having the added responsibility can prepare you for understanding that your life will never be your own again!

New babies (or puppies) throw us curves from time to time— curves that we need to be prepared to handle. This is why before getting pregnant, couples should examine their lives to see how and where this added responsibility will fit in.

Yes, it's different when it's an actual baby. Your lives are going to completely revolve around that little baby—something that doesn't happen when it's a dog. But the fact remains that the responsibility of taking care of a helpless new being is pretty much the same. If you or your spouse are too involved in your careers at the moment, or too wrapped up in your social life, perhaps it's best that you wait a little while later before getting pregnant. The bottom line is that you need to be absolutely sure that both of you are prepared to become parents before actually doing so. You owe it to each other, and you owe it to your future baby.

79.

Love Maintenance

Think about your new relationship as if it's a new car. At first, it's exciting! You take it out all the time and experience a thrill. But what happens when after a while, that oil light comes on? You're past due for an oil change—and maybe a tune-up—but you have so many other pressing matters to attend to that you let it go.

You can still drive around town, but soon you're going to notice that something isn't right. Your car isn't running as smoothly as it used to. Again, you hope that the problem will go away, so you ignore the flashing warning signal.

What happens then? Your car troubles don't magically disappear. They get worse. Pretty soon, you find yourself stranded on the side of the road, calling a mechanic. If only you had dealt with the problems back when they presented themselves.

Like an automobile, a relationship requires frequent tune-ups and inspections. It can also stand a little preventative maintenance to ensure that neither of you end up stuck on the side of the road somewhere alone, feeling helpless, insecure, and angry.

Every marriage needs preventative maintenance. Why is it that we find time to deal with our finances, our jobs, our friends—and our cars—but we don't put in the same amount of effort tuning up our marriages? If your relationship somehow falls out of whack, don't wait for the warning lights to flash furiously. Begin some preventative maintenance as soon as the signals are there.

Let's face it—certain problems just don't go away. You have to tend to them, deal with them, and eventually solve them. Car metaphors notwithstanding, if you suddenly feel your relationship veering off the road, it's up to you to grab hold of the wheel before it runs off course completely!

80.

Things to Say

Speech is a powerful tool and can be extremely effective in a relationship. Finding—and using—the right words can improve your relationship immensely.

Some of us are the strong, silent types and don't always know what to say to our partners—or how to say it. We don't have a way with words, or the creativity and imagination to come up with spectacular, complimentary prose.

You don't have to be a prolific writer or an experienced public speaker to learn the right words to say to please your spouse. Think about the things that you might like to hear from your spouse every so often, and you have yourself the beginnings of a list already. It isn't difficult or complicated to find the perfect words to exemplify your feelings. In fact, it's the simple words we use that are often the most effective. The trick is learning to use them at just the right moment or in just the right situation.

Here are some simple things that you can say, but when and where you choose to say them is up to you. Here's a hint: Saying them at the least obvious moments will lend them extra punch.

- I love you.
- You are very special to me.
- I missed you today.
- What can I do to help you?
- I was wrong. Please forgive me.
- You have my full attention.
- You are so beautiful (or handsome)!
- You are so sexy!
- I'm proud of you.
- Thank you.

What do you really think about your partner? What are your favorite memories of times shared? Tell them. Tell them how much they mean to you. Compliment them as often as possible. Don't worry about using the "right" words—remember that, above all, it is the emotion behind the words that really matters.

81.
Practice Makes Perfect

You've found the perfect person to share your life with. Happily ever after, right? Let's hope so.

The truth is that maintaining love and passion in a marriage takes practice. When you agreed to marry, you signed up for a very important job: loving someone forever. In the beginning, it can be easy to express your love often and freely, but as time goes by, some of us become lazy. We become so comfortable in the relationship that we don't feel the need to express our love or practice loving each other.

Love is a language that needs to be practiced in order to achieve perfection. Begin by practicing some of the ways that you can express your love: physical touch, quality time, words of acknowledgment, acts of service, and gift-giving. Learn which of these ways your partner responds to best, and then practice expressing your love in those ways.

Practice the art of listening to each other. Nothing keeps the romance alive like being heard. Appreciate your partner's point of view. When your partner shares with you, let him or her know that what he or she has to say is important. Give your undivided attention.

Recognize that you have a lot of years ahead of you. Keeping the love alive in your marriage will require a lot more than watching a few sunsets together. Though it's difficult to achieve perfection in anything, by practicing your expressions of love, you may just reach that perfect happy ending.

82.

The Best Gifts Ever

Gifts given from the heart are the perfect way to keep the spark kindled in your relationship. Gifts from the heart are not always presents or trinkets purchased at a store; they can be handwritten poems of love, creative, handmade crafts or artwork, or the simple act of cooking a favorite meal for your spouse. They can be bestowed upon loved ones any time of the year—or week, as the case may be.

These small tokens speak volumes to their recipients. They communicate love, affection, sensitivity, and understanding. A gift from the heart is any unique way that you can think of to offer your love to your spouse. The gift itself need not be the "perfect" item, but rather an expression of your emotions for the one who is "perfect" for you.

To find gifts from the heart, visit your local library. Find a sonnet that expresses your feelings for your spouse. Think unconventional and be silly! Surprise your love with a day of bungee-jumping or pack a picnic lunch for two and head to your favorite park. Draw your spouse a bubble bath, and then bring champagne or wine to sip as he or she relaxes.

Have a gourmet meal prepared for your spouse upon arrival home from work (or pick one up ready-made from your favorite restaurant). Make a tape or CD of all your favorite songs for your spouse to listen to in the car.

The challenge is to select gifts that communicate the way that you feel or show your concern and consideration for helping your spouse get through a hectic day or rough time. You can always go to the store and buy some perfume, jewelry, golf clubs, or tennis rackets, but showering each other with gifts from the heart will be much more appreciated. You can count on it!

83.

Keeping the Romance Alive

When people hear of couples renewing their vows, what usually comes to mind is an older couple reconfirming their love and commitment to one another for all the world to see. While this rekindling is an excellent way to reaffirm a couple's relationship, it isn't a practice that should only be left to long-married couples. Every couple can benefit from this, as it's easy to become lazy in even a young marriage. The day-to-day work and living experiences that a couple shares can be overwhelming for anyone. Whether you're married for years or just months, every marriage can use a little boost.

It's not just about repeating your vows, either. There are many ways that a couple—even a newly married couple—can reignite the romance and the excitement in their marriage. Whichever way you and your spouse find that reinforces your relationship and gives you the strength and desire to continue head-on into the future will certainly be as meaningful and momentous as an exchange of vows.

Why not renew your vows with your spouse on your first anniversary? Plan for it ahead of time—make it an opportunity to recognize each other's ongoing commitment to sharing a life, and to appreciate the unconditional efforts made by each of you every single day to make the relationship continue successfully.

If you still have your vows from your wedding, you can exchange the same ones again. If not, try writing new vows. Lives can change drastically in just one year, and you may find that you and your spouse have new things to vow.

Renewal is healthy in any relationship, but the truth is that many couples preoccupied with busy lives, careers, families, and social engagements often (innocently) take their relationships for granted. This can lead to a false sense of security in a loving relationship. Marriages need day-to-day, week-to-week, and month-to-month confirmation that everything is on track and that everything will be all right in the future. Imagine how wonderful it will be to tell your spouse all over again how grateful you are to have found him or her— not to mention how wonderful it will be to hear the same loving words back!

84.

Surprise!

The element of surprise in a relationship can work wonders. Nothing sends a person's adrenaline soaring like a little unexpected fun!

There are many opportunities a person can have to surprise a partner. Simple, sweet declarations of love at unexpected moments can bring feelings of warmth, security, and joy to the one you love.

However you choose to surprise your spouse, remember that a little mystery, intrigue, and suspense go a long way! Placing strategically hidden love notes, silly messages, or sweet poems throughout the house for your spouse to find is a sure way to elicit a smile from your lover—even where you're not around. An unexpected note discovered accidentally that says "Hello," "I love you," or "I miss you," can help someone left behind from a business trip feel less insecure and lonely while you're away.

85.
Caring Couples

We all recognize that a relationship needs nurturing in order to flourish. One of the most valuable ways that we can achieve growth in our relationships is through the simple act of caring.

Caring and thoughtfulness are what remove us from our isolated world of selfish concerns and let us put someone else's needs above our own. Husbands and wives entrust everything to one another—their emotions, love, respect—in the hope that their relationship will be valued and secure. Sadly, many couples think that the love they feel on their wedding day will carry them through life, regardless of what they do or how they behave. But couples who stop caring stop meeting the most vital emotional needs of their spouse.

Married couples have a responsibility to meet each other's emotional needs. Men and women have very different needs, and it's important to recognize that all are important to us in some way. As husbands and wives, it's our job to determine our partners' most powerful needs and then meet them to the best of our ability. Don't assume that your partner's needs are the same as yours, either, or you'll set yourself up for failure.

How do you know if you are being caring? You have to ask! Get feedback about the quality of your effort and whether or not the quantity is right. Often, a small amount of effort goes a long way.

Each husband and wife brings a unique perspective to their marriage. They each have their own personalities, opinions, and methods of operation. Though thousands of personality traits all come together in a marriage between two unique individuals, their marriage can ultimately be successful when the core of their relationship is founded on caring. A marriage of two people who put each other first, care for each other without reservations, share a mutual concern for the other's well-being, and give each other room for personal growth is a marriage that flourishes.

86.

Sharing Couples

It's a given that married couples have to share. Possessions, responsibilities, caring for the children—they're all part of the commitment of marriage. But more important than anything else, sharing feelings is a priority.

It's easy to share your thoughts. It's not so easy, however, to share your feelings, but there are ways you can try.

Recognize the difference between thoughts and emotional (not physical) feelings. Learn and use the "I think versus I feel" rule. If you can substitute the words "I think" for "I feel" in a sentence, then you have expressed a thought and not a feeling.

Label your feelings (hurt, anger, rejection). Then describe the feelings in writing—this will help your spouse experience your feelings, to some degree.

Accept that feelings are neither right nor wrong. It's the behavior that results from the feeling that has moral issues. Also accept that feelings come and go and feelings change—sometimes quickly!

Never judge yourself or your spouse because of feelings. Rejecting a feeling is rejecting the person feeling it. Avoid saying things like, "You shouldn't feel that way." And never make decisions based on feelings.

Get into the habit of sharing your feelings with your spouse as often as possible. Make it a mutual practice, and soon it will become standard operating procedure for your relationship.

87.

The Heat of the Moment

Given that once you're married, you're more *intimate* than ever, how can you learn to overlook what's become routine in your lives and still manage to fall even more deeply in love? By breathing fresh life into your same old love, that's how!

It's very easy for married couples to fall into a rut. Get home from work, grab a bite to eat, sit on the sofa, and watch television. Or on the weekends: Wake up, go out for breakfast, read the paper, and then separate to run errands or participate in different activities.

How do you kick it up a notch? Think small, first of all. Many times, it's the smaller things—the little changes that we make—that can result in the most satisfaction. Review the routine that you already enjoy with your spouse and then dream up ways to make it better.

Does she insist on a morning kiss? Give her one—in the shower.

Does he enjoy dinner and a show on Saturday nights? Try dinner and a motel room next Saturday night instead.

Been spending your Sundays driving around town, looking at houses? Next Sunday take that same drive—and look for somewhere you can "park" for a while instead.

Trying new things is a great way to keep your relationship exciting and satisfying. You may think that you know everything about each other, but surely there are things about your spouse that you don't know. Asking your partner what desires they have—and fulfilling them—can be a powerful act of generosity and a great way to shake things up!

Above all, keep it fun. So what if you don't achieve perfection? You'll both certainly have fun trying!

88.

Start Your Own Traditions

Beginning your own family traditions—and not just around holidays—can mark the passing years of your life together. Whether it's joining the neighborhood caroling choir for their Christmas rounds each year, or beginning the practice of a potluck brunch on New Year's Day, these types of celebrations will give you and your spouse—and eventually your children—a foundation to build upon for future generations.

Consider the things that mean the most to the both of you: gathering together for family meals, vacationing in the same place each Memorial Day weekend, or just spending the day at home together every Easter Sunday. Practicing the same thing consistently every year will give you many enjoyable experiences to look forward to as the year goes by and bring you closer together in their preparations.

When you have children, following family traditions takes on a whole new meaning. You'll experience a sense of accomplishment and success every year as you become involved in the organizing and planning of your traditions together. Including little children whenever possible adds to the dimension of the tradition, as well. Giving each family member a share of the responsibilities makes everyone feel appreciated and important.

Even if it's just the two of you—make it your mission to consistently be looking out for new ways to begin family traditions. There are many ways to create rituals outside the holidays, too. Spend the first weekend of each New Year away from home. Or plan a family reunion at the end of August each year and invite all of your relatives. Even if you've only experienced something once—if you enjoyed it and look forward to doing it again, then call it your family tradition, and stick with it each year!

The key to successful family traditions is togetherness. No matter what you choose to do together, you're creating a foundation for a lasting marriage.

89.

Magic Love Potions

There's no special potion that keeps romantic love alive. But here are some ideas that you'll sure enjoy trying!

Indulge in some aromatic sensory stimulants. Perfume your bed sheets with sprigs of fresh lavender, a traditional herbal stimulant for love. Or try lavender-stuffed pillows or sachets in your pillowcases.

Light the path to intimacy with scented candles. Food scents such as apple-cinnamon, baked brownie, and vanilla are believed to have the power to turn a person into a love-hungry honey! Other favorite scents include strawberry-cream, sugar cookie, and peach.

Prepare a seductive dessert, using all of the ingredients the so-called love potion gods claim are aphrodisiacs. How about a rich, chocolate cake or mousse with a dash of cinnamon, a few dried rose petals, and some rainwater?

Fill your bedroom with fresh roses (provided your spouse is not allergic)—pink for romance and red for passion. Add a few daffodils, too, which signify deep spiritual love.

Some say precious stones have tremendous sensual power! Hematite will excite you, onyx will strengthen fidelity, malachite near the heart can enrich your relationship, and rose quartz can trigger a physical attraction.

Essential oils like rose, lavender, and jasmine are said to inspire love. Grind your own by mixing the ground flowers with some grapeseed oil and a dash of cinnamon.

Whip up a passion cocktail. Mix a few ounces of passion fruit juice with liqueur and vodka, and strain over ice into a martini glass with a twist of lime. The love gods tell that this passion cocktail served very cold will turn the mood very hot!

90.

For Better or Worse

Every marriage, unfortunately, will go through times of crisis. Some marriages will be strengthened by a crisis; others will end up being destroyed. If you already have a strong marriage, the odds are in your favor that it will withstand crisis. Though there's no way to plan for the unexpected, you can discuss with your partner how you might react in a crisis situation in the unfortunate event that it happens to you.

Crisis happens on all levels. Everyone wishes for a carefree life, devoid of tragedy and sadness, though most families at one time or another will experience some sort of crisis situation and be called upon to deal with it. These are the times that you should be able to count on your spouse, or be counted on by your spouse. When all is said and done, this is what matters most—being there for each other.

Should crisis strike in your life, try following your premeditated plans. Don't worry about smaller concerns—especially when you have such larger issues to deal with. Avoid placing blame on one another in any crisis or emergency situation. Move ahead instead, and work toward getting through the crisis. You can't lean on each other if one of you is placing blame.

Look for occasional distractions. Laughing can help, too—as long as you don't experience guilt for doing so. Hug each other as much as possible. Any type of physical touch can help settle nerves. Hold one another, snuggle together, or just hold hands.

Remember your commitment to each other: for better or worse. This is why they put this vow in most wedding vows—because there will come a time in every marriage where your strength will be tested. If your mate can step up to the plate in the worst of times, rest assured that you exchanged vows with the right person.

Remind yourselves that this crisis won't last forever. It may change things drastically and forever for you both, but no matter how devastating the circumstances you're experiencing, know that you will find happiness again in your lives.

91.

Does Love Conquer All?

Many of the relationships that we cultivate through the course of our lives go through similar patterns. Influenced by transitions in life such as childbirth, promotions, moves, retirement, and aging, marriages pass through stages, each presenting certain challenges that threaten to undermine the relationship.

More than likely, the reason for these changes is not that you and your spouse have fallen out of love. It is usually that the couple has become stuck in one stage of marriage development and has reached an impasse. Learning about the stages through which marriage passes, and how to sail smoothly through the rougher courses, can help you and your spouse come close to that fairy tale ending.

Stage One: Honeymoon Love—We all want the romance to last forever. In fact, we expect it to! In a new love, everything seems perfect at first. We wear rose-colored glasses and life is great. Part of what is happening in this stage of our relationship, the experts tell us, is that our overwhelming feelings of love are the cause of a chemical reaction. Our bodies become flooded with an endorphin called phenoethalymine, which increases our energy levels, our desire, and our positive outlook. It's as if we are "under the influence"! Everything feels right.

Stage Two: Disappointment and Distress—One of the biggest illusions in our culture is that romantic love will last forever once you find the perfect partner—that if you have to work on your relationship, it must not be true love. What pressure! Recognize, as you go through this dangerous stage of disillusionment in your marriage, that there isn't a relationship on this planet that doesn't need attention, maintenance, and work to sustain. Guess what? One reason that you're often feeling irritated by your partner's behavior or hurt from their lack of attention is because your phenoethalymine levels have begun to drop. Because you equated your euphoric feelings from the Honeymoon Stage with your mate, you may begin to blame him or her when you're suddenly not feeling so hot. Anger, blame, and resentment begin to build. If enough distress builds, you may find yourself avoiding your partner and turning to other people or activities to meet your needs. Marriage isn't turning out to be all that you thought it would be.

Stage Three: Acceptance and Transformation—This is the epiphany of all the marriage stages! It's where you not only recognize that your relationship is troubled but that you have the power to turn it around. You understand that having the perfect partner or the perfect marriage is an illusion. You and your spouse can make the conscious choice to find solutions to your problems. You can take control of your relationship rather than sitting back and letting it run you. In this stage, focus on your behavior. Look for warning signs that what you are doing is not helpful to your relationship. Accept the fact that your spouse is not the key to your happiness. The person that you married cannot meet all of your needs all of the time. By the end of this stage, you will hold in your heart the vision of the relationship that you want. You'll work each day toward making it a reality.

Final Stage: True Love—You *can* get here, to this stage of deep respect and real commitment. You'll cherish each other as individuals. You'll have fun again and share the activities, conversations, and intimacies that once brought you joy. This is the stage where you begin to live out your vision of true partnership, unconditional love, and safety, and come to see that your partner, in spite of his or her faults, is your best friend.

It never just happens by itself. If you find yourselves stuck in a motionless stage, get help! Don't throw away your relationship because it has suddenly become difficult. True love is possible—if you are both willing to work at it.

92.

A Better Marriage

On New Year's Eve we often make resolutions to improve our lives. The same theory should be applied to improving your marriage! This December 31, make a list of resolutions to better your marriage. Here are some resolutions to try.

I promise to change my tune—and my tone. When you see your spouse at the end of the day, your first impulse may be to bark out commands or be critical. Instead, stop yourself from saying anything negative and simply go over to him or her and give a kiss hello.

I promise to give big kisses. Many couples, by the time that they're married for a while, forget what it was like to exchange slow, soft, tender kisses. The next time that you kiss your spouse, hold it for an extra count of ten. Go back to the days where you kissed until you thought your lips would fall off—it's unbelievable what a little passionate kissing can do for your relationship!

I promise to devote more time to talking. Couples need to devote more time per day to consciously communicating with their mates if they want to have a meaningful relationship. If you don't make time to talk, you'll end up in a routine of not talking.

I promise to choose my words wisely. Some relatively harmless words that we use when communicating with our mates end up leading straight to trouble. Words like "should" or "I can't" can have a harsh impact when thrown at your partner day after day. Try rephrasing your requests into softer, more effective words. Choose your words wisely to create cooperation instead of conflict.

I promise to soften the situation. It's amazing how we can sometimes treat our mates when they've done something to our dissatisfaction. We end up saying things to our spouses that we would never say to our friends, family members, or even complete strangers! You need to at least treat the person that you love with the same consideration.

I promise to hold hands more. Most people are just dying to be touched. They may not realize it as they're going through the business of their day, but they will definitely realize it the moment that they are caressed, hugged, massaged, or kissed! Hold hands with your honey, caress his or her neck, or just give an impromptu hug when it's least expected.

Be persistent! Make marriage resolutions and stick to them!

93.

What's Your Secret?

There isn't one big secret to having a happy marriage, but there are little secrets to keeping your marriage on the path to happiness. Here are some things that you can do quietly along the way to ensure that your happy, healthy relationship stays on track.

Don't try to change your mate; change yourself. You can't change someone! Instead of trying to change your partner, change your reactions to his or her actions.

Monitor your own personal happiness. Whatever else changes in your life, there will always be one constant: you. In order to ensure that the happiness of your marriage continues, you need to be sure that you yourself are happy. Change your attitude, your thinking, and your capacity to feel satisfied if need be. If you're happy, your marriage will be a happy one, too.

Keep in control. You are in control of your own life. If you're unhappy about something, start transforming yourself into the person that you want to be. Don't blame your mate for your inability to control things. And don't wait until something unpleasant ruins your relationship. It's up to you to take control of your own happiness.

Embrace the flaws. Your mate *will* have flaws! You may not see them or recognize them at first, but they're there. Accepting your mate, flaws and all, is the key to a lasting relationship.

Don't be scared of arguments. There's no doubt about it—it's scary to fight with your spouse. But in fact, certain disagreements can end up building intimacy between couples. Coming to an understanding after a big blowout can do wonders for a relationship. So have that fight—just as long as you make up afterward.

Actions speak louder than words. If you're feeling overwhelming love, grab your mate and kiss him or her passionately. If you're feeling gratitude and appreciation for something he or she did, do something equally fabulous in return. Showing your love or appreciation in caring ways can often be more effective than just saying the words time and again.

Don't take love for granted. As time goes on, take care to remember that seasoned relationships deserve the same respect and care as newlywed relationships.

Pick your battles. Stop arguing endlessly over issues that you disagree on. Just because you both don't see eye to eye on everything doesn't mean that you don't love each other.

Don't lay blame. You'll never solve a problem if you begin by pointing fingers and finding fault with your spouse. You'll end up with a lot of built-up resentment and an unwillingness to reach an agreement. In a partnership such as marriage, you need to learn to solve problems without laying blame.

Keep the flirting alive! Just because you're married doesn't mean that you can't flirt anymore—with each other! The power of a compliment or a few kind, sexy words can be overwhelming! Think back to all of the things that you used to say to your sweetheart when you were dating. Remember how fun flirting with each other was? Get into the practice of it again, and you'll both feel better about yourselves and your relationship.

94.

The "M" Word

Do conversations about money rapidly escalate into accusations and hurt feelings? The truth is that the topic of money is a well-known relationship-buster.

There are good reasons why money is such a charged subject in a marriage, but there are also steps that you can take to work together and sort out your financial problems as a team. Keep in mind that simply having more money isn't the answer. Even wealthy couples fight about money.

Money is about power. We often value ourselves in terms of how much wealth we've accumulated or how high our salaries are. With most couples, there's an imbalance right off the bat. Add to that the fact that men and women traditionally have different attitudes toward money and you've got the potential for a real power struggle.

Constant fighting over money can be avoided. The key to avoiding those fights is coming to terms with your own relationship with money. Get in sync with your partner about your attitudes toward earning and handling money. In a nonjudgmental way, sit down and discuss your spending habits, and make changes or adjustments that you can both live with. It's important that you share the power associated with money and the control that it brings in your relationship. It's also important that both partners share the knowledge of where their money is and what it's doing on a monthly basis. Nobody should be left in the dark with regard to their financial status.

You've chosen to live and work together as a team. Now manage your good fortune like one, too.

95.

Having Kids—

Is the Honeymoon Over?

New parents who are also newly married need to confront the changing expectations that come with having children. Some feel that the marriage should be the same as it was before the children, and when it isn't, something is wrong. Their disappointment can lead to resentment that in turn creates distance in the marriage.

New parents wonder why they are so tired at the end of the day, why they have no time for each other, and why things seem so different now that they have kids. It's simply because the demands of parenting are so great. Recognize that you and your spouse are in this child-rearing thing together, and your relationship can sustain even the most exhausting situations.

Quality time together will be precious and scarce. Time spent as a couple may be virtually nonexistent! But while raising young children is one of the most difficult jobs that an adult will have in his or her lifetime, it should not be accomplished at the expense of a marriage. Truth be told, if parents spent as much time on their marriages as they spend on their children, they would have very happy and healthy marriages. Keep that in mind the next time that you're on the fence about hiring a baby-sitter for the night.

Many couples focus heavily on their children, forgetting the necessity of being close with their spouses. But children are found to do better emotionally in the long run when they grow up in a home where the parents are loving and nurturing to each other. Children learn to respect their parents' relationship, and the family foundation flourishes.

Raising children is complex, to say the least, but it can be very rewarding for both parents and ultimately result in positive changes in their own relationship. Bonding over the responsibilities of a new baby, sharing the joy over their children's achievements—it all brings a happiness and sense of togetherness that a couple might not find elsewhere. After having children, the honeymoon doesn't necessarily have to be over.

96.

Sustaining a
Marriage with Kids

When your plate is full and your list of things to do grows—you must care for your kids, your job, your health, your home—you may find that once in a while, your spouse is going to take a backseat. But it's your partner—the one you often take for granted when life is at its busiest—who ultimately holds the key to nourish and replenish you. As tired as you may be, it's in your best interest to foster a more loving partnership and continue to put in the extra work required for sustaining your marriage.

Set up a time with your spouse to articulate your shared goals and dreams. You're in this relationship for the long haul. Keep that fact close to your heart, even when you can't seem to find the time to be nurturing to your spouse.

Communicate honestly, directly, and as often as possible. Even if your only discussions seem to be had through e-mail these days, keep it going. It's important to communicate to avoid growing apart.

Don't waste precious couple time watching television! When the kids are asleep, use your time constructively. Your marriage will blossom when you scale back the distractions and use the quiet moments you have to be together.

Continue to share hobbies and interests—even when time is limited. Appreciate and acknowledge each other in front of your children, and try not to criticize. Children—even babies—pick up on the mood in a household. Encourage a loving, respectful environment at home and your children will grow up to be loving, respectful people.

Look for ways to lighten each other's load, and spend as much quality time with your family as possible. Your rewards will be endless.

97.

Second Time Around

Are you walking down the aisle for the second time around? If you are, you may be feeling worry and angst like you've never experienced before. Second-time brides and grooms have the worst cases of pre-wedding jitters, largely due to the fact that they're worried about what people will think of them.

Stop worrying! The fact is that more than thirty percent of weddings today involve at least one partner who's been married before. Bridal salons, ring designers, florists, caterers—they're all privy to the fact that more couples today are marrying for the second time. In fact, they often reconfigure their businesses to appeal specifically to *you*.

Your family, your parents, your friends—they all have your best interests at heart. They're overjoyed for you—especially after watching you live through earlier sadness. Ask them to remind you how lucky you are to have found love again when you were so sure that you wouldn't. You can count on supportive friends and family to help get this new phase of your life off to a perfect start.

You're a completely different person now. With the experience of marriage already under your belt, you're at a tremendous advantage this time around. You know what to look out for—what warning signs look like and how they present themselves. You're ready to head toward "forever" again with someone you love deeply.

Surviving the worst and managing to bounce back is going to work in your favor. You are older, wiser, and more experienced. You've lost love and regained it. Now you can use all that you've learned to create a new, lasting relationship.

98.

Kiss and Make Up

Along with all the happy times, every couple is bound to experience rough spots every now and then. While fighting is normal in a relationship, it is definitely not fun. Making up, however, is!

According to many couples who've been through some big ones, when it comes to arguments, making up almost makes all the fighting worthwhile! It's actually a well-known secret to getting your relationship back on track after a fight. From a cool-down walk to makeup passion, there are many effective ways to end an argument. Physical intimacy is the number-one argument-ender, according to married couples. For many, it's a must in order for them to move past the fight. Best of all, it offers a frazzled couple fresh from arguing an immediate opportunity to get close again.

Another way that couples can stop a fight dead in its tracks is to take a little breather. Spend a half hour apart and give tempers a time to cool. Reflect on the argument—but don't return to the negotiating table until your stress and anger levels have subsided. Then talk it through, with each of you agreeing to hear the other one out without interruption. Once you've come to an agreement and everything has been discussed to each other's satisfaction, start hugging and kissing. That immediate physical contact is essential as the dust of your battle is still settling.

Yet another effective way to end an argument is to look for the humor in the situation. Maybe your argument started out about something small and silly and then just took on a life of its own. If you have been battling over something unimportant, try laughing at yourselves.

Whatever ways you and your spouse choose to make up after an argument, the important thing is that you do, indeed, make up. There's an old bit of relationship advice often passed down from generation to generation that is definitely a cliché, but remains absolutely true: Never go to bed angry. If you and your spouse can resolve your differences—even if it means getting to sleep at three in the morning after a fight—your hurt feelings won't fester and linger longer than they should.

99.

Happy Anniversary!

There's nothing like the feeling of celebrating your very first wedding anniversary. What an important milestone in the course of your lives together! Don't let it go by without the pomp and circumstance that it deserves!

Make the event special, no matter what day it falls on. Celebrate in style from the moment that you wake up in the morning until the moment your heads hit the pillows that night. There's no more cause for celebration than a first wedding anniversary, and you shouldn't let a blissful second go by without reflecting on your love for each other.

Gifts made from paper are the traditional way to celebrate a first anniversary. Write your spouse a love letter on the back of your wedding napkin (if any remain), or on the back of a leftover invitation. Scan your favorite wedding photo and create a scrapbook page with a loving message on your computer. Present your honey with an original edition of the daily newspaper from either the date of your wedding or the date that he or she was born. Or find a rare edition of his or her favorite childhood book—with paper, the possibilities are endless! Give tickets to a sporting event or show, a gift certificate to a favorite shop or restaurant, a postcard from where you honeymooned—or a personalized calendar with pictures of the two of you through the years, marked with all your important dates.

Plan the entire day, remembering to include some of the people who are most special to you. Have a party, arrange a dinner, or just share the time together alone. Have your picture taken to commemorate the event—something that you can do together every anniversary for the rest of your lives. Next year, for your second anniversary, the traditional gift is cotton. After that, it goes as follows.

- Third anniversary: leather
- Fourth anniversary: fruit or flowers
- Fifth anniversary: wood
- Sixth anniversary: iron
- Seventh anniversary: wool or copper
- Eighth anniversary: bronze
- Ninth anniversary: pottery
- Tenth anniversary: tin or aluminum
- Twentieth anniversary: china
- Twenty-fifth anniversary: silver

- Fiftieth anniversary: gold
- Seventy-fifth anniversary: diamond

Always treasure your wedding anniversary—whether it's your first, your sixth, or your seventy-fifth! It's a day that deserves special attention—a day that you'll have each year for the rest of your lives that you can dedicate to celebrating your love.

100.

Celebrating Your Marriage

When you first got engaged, you couldn't stop thinking about how wonderful married life was going to be. Then, after the wedding gown and tuxedo were long packed away in storage, after your first joyous wedding anniversary celebration, after a child or two came into your lives, your priorities changed. You just didn't have a whole lot of time for thinking about your marriage anymore.

Regardless of time constraints, successful marriages still need to be celebrated as often as possible. Even if you're consumed with work, diapers, needy relatives, neighbors, or homework, every man and woman involved in a loving relationship should still find time to gush over the marriage.

Try fitting in opportunities to reconnect with your spouse whenever possible during the hustle and bustle of everyday life. Keep in mind that it isn't the traditional, scheduled events in our lives, such as anniversary dinners or Saturday nights out, that bring spouses together or bond them. It's the little bits of stolen time together and the small gestures of love that we make that are the most powerful reminders of our commitment to one another.

Be sure to say the words, and say them often. Tell your spouse that you love him or her and why you fell in love with him or her in the first place. Get into the practice of bestowing gifts on each other—for no reason at all. These do not necessarily have to be expensive gifts, but gifts that make us feel connected and remind us that we're always looking out for each other.

Toast each other! Pour yourselves a glass of wine or champagne every once in a while and exchange tender words and compliments.

Hit the dirt—literally! Plant a new sapling or tree in your yard and watch it grow bigger and stronger each year of your marriage.

Most important, make it a habit to save and savor everything—an "I love you" note left taped to the bathroom mirror or rose petals from that wonderful day you spent together playing hooky from work. Whatever moves you, be sure to preserve it as best you can. Nothing is too silly or too strange to save. It will unlock the warm, happy times that you shared throughout your marriage and give you cause for celebration in the years to come!